D1860021

CLIMBING AND EXPLORATION
IN THE
KARAKORAM HIMALAYAS

Owing to the antiquity and rarity of this book, certain pages are regrettably absent, and readability is compromised due to the blurring of the original text. If you possess any insights regarding the availability of these missing sections, kindly inform us. Your assistance is crucial in ensuring the completion of this significant work for the benefit of future generations.

CLIMBING AND EXPLORATION

IN THE

KARAKORAM HIMALAYAS

WILLIAM MARTIN CONWAY

GYAN

Published by

GYAN

Gyan Publishing House
5, Ansari Road
Daryaganj, New Delhi-110002
Phone: 011-47034999, 9811692060
E-mail: books@gyanbooks.com

Distribution Network
gyanbooks.com
India, USA, Canada, UK, Australia

© Publisher

All rights reserved. No part of this work may be reproduced, stored, adapted, or transmitted in any form or by any means, electronic, mechanical, photocopying, micro-filming, recording or otherwise, or translated in any language, without the prior written permission of the copyright owner and the publisher.

ISBN: **978-93-6920-248-5** (HB)

First Published, 1894

2nd Impression 2025

Printed at: Gyan Press, Delhi.

The book is sold subject to the condition that it shall not, by way of trade or otherwise, be lent, resold, hired out, or otherwise circulated without the prior publisher's written consent.

CLIMBING AND EXPLORATION IN THE KARAKORAM HIMALAYAS
Author: WILLIAM MARTIN CONWAY

CLIMBING AND EXPLORATION
IN THE KARAKORAM-HIMALAYAS

Photo. by Cameron & Smith 70, Mortimer St. W. — Swan Electric Engraving Co.

Yrs
W. M. Conway

CLIMBING AND EXPLORATION

IN THE

KARAKORAM-HIMALAYAS

BY

WILLIAM MARTIN CONWAY

M.A., F.S.A., F.R.G.S.

Vice-President of the Alpine Club; formerly Roscoe Professor of Art in University College, Liverpool, Victoria University

CONTAINING SCIENTIFIC REPORTS

BY

Prof. T. G. BONNEY, D.Sc., F.R.S.; Dr. A. G. BUTLER, F.L.S., F.Z.S.; W. MARTIN CONWAY; W. LAURENCE H. DUCKWORTH, B.A.; Lt.-Col. A. G. DURAND, C.B.; W. BOTTING HEMSLEY, F.R.S.; W. F. KIRBY, F.L.S., F.E.S.; Miss C. A. RAISIN, B.Sc.; and Prof. C. F. ROY, F.R.S.

WITH FRONTISPIECE PORTRAIT OF THE AUTHOR, AND MAPS.

London

T. FISHER UNWIN

PATERNOSTER SQUARE

MDCCCXCIV

CONTENTS.

THE EASTERN HINDU KUSH.

THE EASTERN HINDU KUSH.

By LIEUT.-COLONEL A. G. DURAND, C.B., Military Secretary to the Viceroy of India, late British Agent and Commanding the Troops at Gilgit.

PUBLIC attention has of late years been turned very frequently to the Eastern Hindu Kush region, numerous expeditions have crossed and re-crossed the great table-lands and valleys to the north of the main range, and a voluminous, if occasionally sketchy and unsatisfactory, literature has grown up round the Pamir question. The country to the south of the Eastern Hindu Kush is not so well known generally, although it has been exhaustively explored. It is about this portion of the Hindu Kush region, included in the limits of the Gilgit Agency, directly under its influence, or indirectly connected with it, that I shall treat. For detailed information I would refer any who care to pursue the subject further, to my predecessor in Gilgit, Major Biddulph's exhaustive work, "The Tribes of the Hindu Kush," and to my friend Mr. Knight's most interesting book of travel, "Where Three Empires Meet." I must preface my remarks by pointing out that it is of course impossible for me to enter into the discussion of military and political questions.

To the region in question, which embraces Chitral on the

west, including Yasin, the Gilgit valley from Gakuch in Punial to the Indus at Bunji, Hunza and Nagyr to the north, the Shin republics of the Indus valley as far as Sazin to the south, the Kohistan-i-Malazai, and a portion of the Indus valley Kohistan, has been applied the name of Dardistan. A misleading title, for there is no such country as Dardistan, and there is no one united race to which the name of Dard could be applied. It is said that the people living on the left bank of the Kandia river are called Dards by their neighbours, but after five years of residence in the country, and repeated journeys from one end of it to the other, with the exception of the Indus valley below Chilas, I can safely say that I have never heard the term used. What were the exact limits of the country inhabited by the Dards of the ancient geographers it is probably impossible to say; the name was most likely applied to the races occupying the Indus valley from Ladakh to the Punjab. At present the name has no scientific value, and often repeated inquiries satisfied me that it is quite unknown to the natives.

Many languages and dialects are spoken throughout this region, and many castes exist in it, of which only the most important can be mentioned. Their distribution seems to point to successive waves of conquest. The races are one and all believed to be Aryan, the people of Hunza and Nagyr presenting a strikingly pure type. Burishki, the language of the Yeshkuns, is spoken in the inaccessible Hunza, Nagyr, and Yasin valleys; Shina throughout Astor, Gilgit, Punial, and the lower part of the Ghizr valley; from the Indus valley through Gilgit to Ghizr the proportion of Shins varies from 90 to 35 per cent. of the population; off the main line of advance in Astor, Hunza, Nagyr, and Yasin, the proportion is reversed, and the Yeshkun preponderate, driven back by the advancing tide. The northern portion of the Hunza valley, called Gujhal, is inhabited by immigrants from Wakhan to the north of the Hindu Kush. In Chitral, as Biddulph says, the population is a curious and intricate ethnological puzzle. The bulk of the people appear to belong to an aboriginal race speaking Khowar; the ruling class, the Adamzada, would seem to be drawn from tribes which held Badakhshan, Shignan, Wakhan, and Roshan. These ethnological questions, however, are too intricate to enter into here.

To the west of Chitral lies Kafiristan, of which I cannot speak. Soon I trust that my friend, Mr. G. S. Robertson, will give to the world the wonderful story of his successful exploration of a great part of that fascinating country. For the best part of a year he lived amongst the Kafirs: he is the only European who has ever penetrated the mountain fastnesses of that most interesting race, the only white man who has crossed the Mandal (or Minjan) pass, has traversed the country from the Hindu Kush to the Kunar valley, and who has visited Viron, the most important village in the heart of this hitherto unexplored country. Putting aside Kafiristan, the region of which I am speaking is still of great interest. It is some 200 miles in width from the Dorah pass, leading from Chitral into Badakhshan to the Indus at Bunji, and 150 miles in depth from the crest of the Hindu Kush to Sazin, where the Indus takes its great bend to the south. Numerous passes from the Shimshal on the east to the Dorah on the west lead into it over the great mountain barrier, and from it roads run to India through the Kunar and Indus valleys, and to Kashmir by Astor and the Gurais valley, roads along which centuries ago flowed the great tide of Buddhist pilgrimage, and caravans of the merchandise of Central Asia. The region may be roughly divided into two main water systems—that of the Chitral river, which, uniting the waters from the Baroghil, Arkari, and Dorah valleys, falls into the Kabul river close to Jelalabad, and joins the Indus above Attock—and that of the Gilgit river, which, after receiving the waters of the Yasin, Ishkúman, and Hunza valleys, falls into the Indus at Bunji. The Indus drains the whole region. The water parting between these two systems is the range joining the Hindu Kush to the Hindu Raj, the latter being the northern watershed of the Indus valley, between Bunji and Chitral.

It is difficult for any one who has not traversed the country to realise what a road in the heart of the Hindu Kush means. When I first visited Gilgit, five years ago, there was not a yard of what we should call a road in the whole region, and only one permanent bridge, that over the Chitral river at Chitral itself. Narrow paths—so narrow that often while the rider's boot on one side brushed the cliff, his outer foot overhung a precipice—followed the course of the streams. Often in the course of one short march the path ascends a thousand feet or more to avoid crossing some precipitous cliff, and the repeated ascents and descents render riding a weariness to the flesh. Frequently the path is carried across the face of a cliff on roughly constructed galleries, upheld by shaky timbers jammed into interstices in the rock. In many of the valleys, when the summer sun melts the accumulations of snow, and the mighty glaciers pour down their flooded torrents, the lower paths become impassable for animals. For months at a time all animal traffic is suspended, and men on foot alone, following giddy tracks skirting gigantic precipices, can with difficulty find their way from valley to valley. Three years ago, for instance, when an impending attack by the Hunza-Nagyr tribesmen on Chalt, our frontier outpost thirty miles north of Gilgit, forced me to move troops to the frontier, it was impossible for me to take a mule battery through with the infantry. The road runs along the Hunza river, through one of the wildest gorges in the Hindu Kush; great cliffs rise sheer out of the water, and tower thousands of feet above you. The heat in June, when we passed through the gorge, is terrific; it always seemed to me a fitting approach to the entrance gate of hell. Eight times in one march had the mules to be unladen, and guns, ammunition, and baggage carried across cliffs by the men. One cliff presented such difficulties that even unladen mules could not cross it, and we were forced to swim them over the river below it, and to re-cross them above it. Again in March last, when moving reinforcements to Chilas in the Indus valley, two marches were impassable to unladen mules, and I was obliged to move down the guns on coolies. Such were the roads all through this region five years ago. Now a good mountain road is complete to Gilgit, the Indus is bridged at Bunji, a passable road leads to Chilas, and the communications generally are improving.

But if the roads are wild and unpleasant for riders troubled with nerves, the scenery to which they give access surpasses in grandeur any that it has been my lot to admire. Gilgit is in the heart of the region where the mountains attain perhaps the greatest average height in the world. Within seventy miles are eight mountains with an elevation of from 24,000 to 26,000 feet, while range after range averages from 18,000 to 20,000 feet. As a rule, however, the wonderful panorama is hidden from sight, for the valleys in which the roads run are very narrow, and the lower hills shut out the view of the great mountains behind. From Gilgit itself the great Rakipushi, 25,000 feet high though it is, and distant but a few miles, is invisible, and only three peaks of lesser importance, "three silent pinnacles of aged snow," relieve the monotony of the view. To one accustomed to the comparatively pigmy hills of Europe, and to the beauty of outline and exquisite variety of colouring of the Swiss and Italian mountains, this portion of the Hindu Kush at first causes a feeling almost of disappointment. The Kashmir mountains, through which the traveller passes on his way north, are clothed in grand fir forests, are covered with vegetation, and are generally soft of outline, compared to the mountains bordering the Indus. The traveller, after leaving Kashmir, each day gets into a more barren region, till at last, with the exception of the patches of cultivation in the valleys, and the scattered forests which begin at an elevation of 7,000 feet, no sign of vegetation meets the eye. On all sides rise bare precipitous mountains, wild in outline, depressing in colouring, repeating with a deadly monotony the same tones of dull grey and yellow, darkening to browns and purples in the shadow. It is only on the rare occasions when rain falls that the colouring, which is obliterated by bright sunlight, shows out. Then the mountain-sides are clothed in delicate reds and browns and soft shades of green, and through the light veil of falling rain, range after range stretches away with exquisitely softened outlines;

and when the dark storm-clouds in spring sweep down the valleys, lurid reds and great washes of purple glorify the silent hills.

Gradually the feeling of vastness gains upon one, as the eye almost tires from ever following from base to crest the severe lines of the enclosing hills, above which occasionally a solitary peak of snow rises majestically into the blue. Splendid panoramas unfold themselves to the traveller crossing some high pass, such as the Banok La, 16,000 feet high, over which the road from Astor to Skardo passes, and around him stretch endless circles of eternal snow. But the height to which it is necessary to ascend generally dwarfs the great peaks, and it is only when from some favourable point a view is obtained of one of the great mountains, complete from foot to summit, that the colossal scale on which Nature has here worked is realised.

Then, indeed, the grandeur is overpowering, and the impression of immensity stamps itself indelibly and almost oppressively on the mind. Finally the eye becomes habituated to the vast proportions, and so accustomed to dwelling on bare and gigantic outlines and monotonous colouring, that the traveller on his return through Kashmir finds that the scenery which had enchanted him on his outward journey with its wild beauty, the valleys through which the road runs hemmed in by cliffs hundreds of feet high, and by fir-clad slopes, the rushing rivers flowing under banks clothed with thickets of white lilac and hazel, all seem modelled on a scale of fairy-like minuteness, and the eye wanders in almost startled pleasure on the ever-changing scene, the varied colouring, and the delightful verdure of the landscape.

There are but few points from which the exceptional views of the greater mountains can be obtained. The finest I have ever seen are those of Nanga Parbat from the Bunji plain, of Rakipushi from Hunza, and Tirich Mir from the Arkari valley in Chitral. Seen from the Bunji plain, Nanga Parbat, 26,000 feet high, fills up the southern end of the valley. The dead grey sloping plain, the bare precipices of hill to right and left, lead up to the narrowing head of the valley hemmed in by fir-clad and snow-tipped hills, and, above all, towering thousands of feet over the Hatu Pir, which itself rises in the foreground in one precipitous wall 6,000 feet sheer out of the plain, majestic and solitary, with no other mountains near to dwarf it, looms the grand mass of Nanga Parbat, 15,000 feet of unbroken snow and ice.

The view of Rakipushi from Hunza is again superb. Standing below the picturesque fort you look across the valley, barely a couple of miles wide, the river running a thousand feet below in a deep gorge. Direct out of the valley in one magnificent sweep of 18,000 feet from the river rises Rakipushi, the lower slopes for thousands of feet bare as usual, covered at their base only by terrace after terrace of cultivation, by endless orchards of apricot, apple, and pear, above them a few patches of dense forest, and then in summer 12,000 to 14,000 feet of snow in one vast pile below which huge glaciers push down almost into the valley. A sight once seen never to be forgotten.

If the country is interesting, so are the people. The Shins, I believe, are a dying race, the Botogah Glen in Chilas, which fifty years ago is said to have turned out 1,200 fighting men, lately furnished a sixth of that number;

in the Indus valley they are decreasing in numbers, and seem to be in danger of being gradually supplanted by more vigorous immigrants from the lower Indus valley; in Gilgit they strike one as unenterprising and wanting in stamina. Throughout the whole region under review I should say the races with some exceptions are naturally peaceful. There is none of the fiery dash of the Pathan, their inter-tribal fights have never been very costly in life. But as I always expected, and as we found in the Hunza-Nagyr expedition, they are stubborn and gallant foes when entrenched. Good cragsmen with a natural talent for making the most of a defensive position, which centuries of fitful warfare has perfected, they are difficult enemies to deal with. That they can "take a licking," as a boy would say, and bear but little malice, that they appreciate fair play, and can recognise the desire we have to prevent oppression, is shown by the state of Hunza and Nagyr. Not a single shot was fired after the final engagement which broke the power of the tribesmen, officers traversed the country from end to end with nominal escort, and within a few months Mr. Conway's party wandered unguarded through the country.

Except in the Indus valley there is no fanaticism. In Yasin, Punial, and Hunza the people are chiefly Maulai, belonging to that heretical Mahommedan sect, the head of which till lately was H. H. Agha Khan, of Bombay. Inheritors, I believe, of the tenets of the "assassin," the followers of Richard I.'s opponent, who was, if I remember right, in our school days called "the Old Man of the Mountain," these schismatics are looked on with horror by orthodox Mahommedans. They scoff at the Koran, say no prayers, drink wine, practically worship the head of the sect, and are said only to be bound to thorough obedience to their "Pirs" or priests. Their religion, such as it is, sits but lightly on them. The Nagyr people are Shiahs; in Chitral both of the great Mahommedan sects are represented, the rulers being Sunni. But nowhere do you find bigotry, except in the Indus valley, which was converted by Mullas from Swat. I well remember my old friend the late Mehtar of Chitral soundly rating one of his sons who was Governor of a province for attempting to interfere with the religious opinions of some of his subjects. He held, from motives of self-interest only, the broad view that so long as his subjects were law-abiding and paid their dues, their religion was no business of his.

The people as a rule are cheery and pleasant. Only in Chilas, that home of rascally cut-throats, whose raids and brutal murders were the curse of the border, until they filled the cup of their iniquity by a treacherous attempt to destroy my friend Mr. Robertson, who was visiting Gor at the people's invitation—an escapade which led to the posting of troops in Chilas itself,—only here do you find scowling faces and a semi-Pathan inclination to murder.

That the rulers have been bloodthirsty is unfortunately true; it must be so in semi-savage Mahommedan states. Sir Alfred Lyall's well-known lines in "The Amir's Soliloquy" always used to ring in my head when talking to the old Mehtar of Chitral:

> "The virtues of God are pardon and pity,
> They never were mine,
> They have never been ours in a country
> All stained with the blood of our kin,
> Where the brothers embrace on the warfield,
> And the reddest sword must win."

The old Mehtar was a typical mountain chief, tall, handsome, distinguished-looking, with a princely bearing, and a dignified courtesy to his guests; he was relentless, cruel as death, a past-master in dissimulation, and steeped to the lips in the blood of his brothers and relations. But he ruled his country. I remember when there was a delay in some posts reaching me, his tracing out the culprit, and what difficulty I had to prevent his selling the wretched man and all his family into slavery. There was no such thing as robbing the king's guest with impunity. I and others repeatedly travelled through the country without escort and generally unarmed.

The Chitralis, the sons of "the land of mirth and murder," as we christened it, in opposition to "the land of gold and apricots," as the Nagyr people call their country, are a short, active race, devoted to polo, passionately fond of dancing and of song, and seem unable to pass a flower without gathering it and sticking it in their small turbans. Their rulers, having no jails, as one of them explained to me, habitually sold any evildoer into slavery. As slaves the Chitralis were much valued across the Hindu Kush for their often proved fidelity. To this day our friend and ally the Amir of Afghanistan has, I believe, Chitrali retainers in most trusted positions immediately about his person, The Chitralis, and indeed all the Hindu Kush people, will sit up all night listening to the maddeningly monotonous music of their pipe and drum bands, watching the dancing boys, or joining in the dance themselves. The infliction it is to be camped near one of their chiefs must be endured to be fully appreciated.

The Hunza people much resemble them in character, but

are of finer physique, and probably better men. The Nagyr people are more subdued: this they and their neighbours attribute to the depressing effect of their climate in winter. Crushed under the great range which rises to the south, their side of the valley is almost sunless for weeks together; the cold is terrible, so they spend nearly all their time during the winter in their dark and gloomy homes, and the dreariness of such an existence reacts on their character.

Throughout the whole region there is not one single town, and no bazaars in the Eastern sense, with the exception of a small one at Gilgit and another at Astor. The little trade that exists is done by pedlars, chiefly men from Koli and Palas in the Indus valley. Except in Gilgit and in one or two instances in Chitral the people live in fortified villages—an arrangement till lately necessary, owing to the unsettled state of the country. These forts are of very solid construction, the outer walls from 10 feet to 15 feet thick, being built of stone and mud st ngthened with solid timbers. The houses are huddled together within them, in many cases built one on the top of the other. There are as a rule no windows; light comes in by the door, and when that is closed, through a square hole in the roof serving the double purpose of chimney and window. There is a certain amount of rude carving, which has a very good effect, on the doors and uprights which support the roof.

Cultivation is dependent on irrigation, for the tract below 8,000 feet is practically rainless. Much ground has, owing to the constant wars and consequent depopulation, fallen out of use, and it has been one of our most grateful tasks to increase the facilities for cultivation of the people by opening disused water channels, and in Hunza and Nagyr by constructing new ones where the engineering difficulties were too great for the people to surmount.

Travelling constantly from end to end of this region, as a warden of the marches is bound to do, I have had many opportunities of observing the people, and of hearing strange and old-world tales. I found that the banshee wails round the towers of a fort in Chitral before the death of the king, that fairies are still seen floating through the air in troops of horse and foot to their home in Tirich Mir, horses are hag-ridden and found with witches' stirrups in their manes, children are carried off, men have passed days in the fairies' company, and that two generations ago a Mehtar of Chitral married a fairy bride. Old age comes to the fairy folk, and some of them, as in Europe, have their feet set on the wrong way. In Chitral they are converted to Mahommedanism and have a praying-place where, on Fridays, they assemble, and the belated Chitrali hears a ghostly call to prayer and the murmur of a great host joining in the prescribed devotions. But in other parts, where the prophet's religion has only been observed for a few generations, they are still unregenerate; and surely their state is the more gracious. Fairy drums are, or were till lately, on the roof of every chief's castle and sounded to war. Fairies inspired women, and under their influence these seers foretold the fate of dynasties, and the result of wars. In the Bagrot valley, twenty miles from Gilgit, I was present when a Dainyal—for so these women are called—after inhaling the smoke of the sacred cedar, went through her mystic dance and prophesied smooth things for the British rule. The ceremony of initiation I did not see—luckily, perhaps. When a woman announces that she is inspired by the fairies, she is made to go through the usual dance with an acknowledged Dainyal. Then a goat is brought in and decapitated, and the novice seizes the neck and drinks the pumping blood. If she can do this she is received as a Dainyal; if not, no attention is paid to her prophecies, and the people tell you that she invariably goes mad.

Relics of dead faiths abound, curious ceremonies usher in the new year and the seasons of seedtime and harvest. The ruler turns the first furrow, scatters the first handful of seed mixed with gold-dust in token of plenty, and offers sacrifice to the gods. Traces of tree worship meet you; the cedar, sacred in Kafiristan, is sacred throughout the whole region; you are incensed with its burning twigs on entering remote villages; the women still cast its boughs in offering on the deserted altar of the half-forgotten village god. Sacred fires blaze on the mountain-sides at certain seasons, and recall the fact that the home of the so-called "fire worship" was but across the Hindu Kush.

Buddhism has left its mark: there is a Buddhist tope not far from Gilgit, which I never had time to explore, Buddhist altars by every path; a great Buddha in the preaching attitude is carved high on the face of a rock three miles from Gilgit, and at the foot of the flagstaff, on which now flies the British flag in the garden of the residency at Gilgit, lies the pedestal of a statue with the socket holes for the feet. But there is an entire absence of sculptured inscriptions throughout the whole region. We have searched far and wide, but not one solitary inscription has been found except one in Chitral, which was copied by Sir W. Lockhart's party, and had reference to a Chinese invasion. That a higher civilisation prevailed in Gilgit formerly the Buddhist remains attest, and the long lines of deep square-cut holes in the rock, in which must have been inserted the supports for large water channels, probably of wood, from which water was drawn to cultivate the hundreds of acres of terraced land which now lie hopelessly dry and barren, far out of reach of the life-giving supply. The present inhabitants of the country have neither the tools nor the skill to undertake such a work, but it is not too much to hope that an era of peace and prosperity is dawning for them in which such works will again be undertaken with success.

I think I have said enough to show that the southern region of the Eastern Hindu Kush is one full of interest. For five years I have lived in it in peace and war, the fascination of its desolate grandeur is still upon me, the memories of solitary days spent in the heart of its glorious mountains can never fade, nor can the kindly feelings towards the cheery and manly inhabitants of its sequestered valleys.

LIST OF MEASURED ALTITUDES.

LIST OF MEASURED ALTITUDES.

Date.	Time.	Place.	Boiling Point. Fahr.	Barometer reduced to 32° Fahr.	Air Temperature. Fahr.	Gilgit. Barometer reduced to 32° Fahr.	Gilgit. Air Temperature. Fahr.	Leh. Barometer reduced to 32° Fahr.	Leh. Air Temperature. Fahr.	Altitude deduced by comparison with Gilgit (4,890 ft.).	Altitute deduced by comparison with Leh (11,503 ft.).	Mean Altitude.
May 11	4.30 p.m.	Sinakar	199°·7	23·38	67°	24·96	79°	19·66	49°	6,940	6,900	6,920
June 3	6.20 p.m.	"		23·17	73°	24·97	80°	19·74	57°			
May 12	2 p.m.	Bulchi Camp		197°·4	22·24	67°	24·88	79°	19·63	46°	8,126	8,103	8,110
" 13	1 p.m.	Dirran Camp	195°·25	21·21	53°	25·02	79°	19·68	45°			
" 14	12.30 p.m.	"	195°·3	21·24	59°	25·06	79°	19·71	59°			
" 15	6.30 p.m.	"	195°·4	21·32	52°	24·91	74°	19·65	54°			
" 16	4 p.m.	"	195° 3	21·23	60°	24·89	79°	19·70	66°	9,522	9,486	9,500
" 20	4 p.m.	"		21·20	60°	24·97	79°	19·73	62°			
" 21	1 p.m.	"		21·08	70°	24·82	79°	19·69	61°			
" 17	noon	Bari Rung		*18·19	60° ?	24·99	79°	19·81	64°	13,941	14,013	13,980
" 18	10.30 a.m.	Kumar Camp	195°·7	*21·44	70°	25·04	73°	19·85	60°	9,430	9,364	9,400
" 18	5 p.m.	Uchubagan Camp	189°·8	*18·91	46°	24·93	78°	19·75	65°	12,650	12,765	12,700
" 19	8 a.m.	Uchubagan Pass		*16·73	55° ?	25·14	68°	19·84	55°	16,300	16,264	16,280
" 19	noon	Serpent's Tooth		*15·98	55° ?	25·01	79°	19·83	64°	17,583	17,577	17,580
" 22	2 p.m.	Gargo Camp		19·75	50°	24·83	79°	19·60	57°			
" 23	2 p.m.	"		19·66	54°	24·78	79°	19·56	60°			
" 23	4 p.m.	"		19·64	57°	24·77	79°	19·55	60°			
" 24	7 p.m.	"		19·60	45°	24·76	67°	19·58	55°			
" 25	6 p.m.	"		19·88	41°	24·96	74°	19·59	61°	11,320	11,351	11,340
" 26	7 a.m.	"		19·80	38°	24·96	68°	19·70	45°			
" 27	8.45 p.m.	"		19·96	50°	25·07	69°	19·74	50°			
" 28	6.30 a.m.	"		19·96	36°	25·07	68°	19·75	40°			
" 26	3.30 p.m.	Birchwood Station		18·38	50°	24·96	79°	19·59	63°	13,620	13,323	13,470
" 28	5 p.m.	Windy Camp		19·07	45°	24·96	76°	19·67	60°			
" 28	5.30 p.m.	"	190°		41°	24·96	76°	19·67	59°			
" 29	6 p.m.	"		18·87	38°	24·87	74°	19·66	49°	12,580	12,636	12,610
" 30	11.30 a.m.	"		18·78	51°	24·89	79°	19·74	54°			

* Readings marked with an asterisk were taken with an aneroid recently corrected by comparison with the Mercurial Barometer.

Date.	Time.	Place.	Boiling Point. Fahr.	Barometer reduced to 32° Fahr.	Air Temperature. Fahr.	Gilgit. Barometer reduced to 32° Fahr.	Gilgit. Air Temperature. Fahr.	Leh. Barometer reduced to 32° Fahr.	Leh. Air Temperature. Fahr.	Altitude deduced by comparison with Gilgit (4,890 ft.).	Altitude deduced by comparison with Leh (11,508 ft.).	Mean Altitude.
May 31	8 a.m.	Breakfast Place		17·07	40°	24·87	68°	19·74	48°	15,270	15,475	15,370
,, 31	noon	Sulphur Camp		16·84	38°	24·81	79°	19·69	61°	15,600	15,763	15,680
June 1	8 a.m.	,, ...		17·01	27°	25·03	77°	19·77	56°			
,, 1	11 a.m.	Left Moraine		18·52	59°	25·02	89°	19·69	60°	13,540	13,270	13,400
,, 1	6.30 p.m.	Burchi		20·10	45°	24·91	83°	19·71	52°	11,050	11,104	11,080
,, 2	11.20 a.m.	,, ...		20·09	51°	25·03	89°	19·84	59°			
,, 2	6.40 p.m.	Burchi Moraine Station		19·77	46°	25·09	80°	19·77	54°	11,600	11,500	11,550
,, 9	5.30 a.m.	Nomal		24·49	61°	24·82	77°	19·61	54°	5,290	5,390	5,340
,, 9	6 p.m.	Chalt		23·61	75°	24·74	85°	19·61	56°	6,266	6,406	6,340
,, 10	4 p.m.	Gulmet		23·61	70°	24·71	89°	19·56	57°	6,376	6,442	6,410
,, 10	6.15 p.m.	,, ...		23·38	68°	24·72	85°	19·56	57°			
,, 11	6 p.m.	,, ...		23·54	64°	24·79	85°	19·61	59°			
,, 12	8 p.m.	Tashot		23·17	63°	24·97	79°	19·62	58°	7,046	6,914	6,980
,, 12	noon	River bank below Tashot ...		*23·55	70° ?	24·96	89°	19·72	58°	6,592	6,568	6,580
,, 13	7 a.m.	Top of zigzags near Fakkar ...		*22·75	64° ?	24·93	77°	19·64	58°	7,518	7,443	7,480
,, 13	8 a.m.	Shaiyar		*22·91	65° ?	24·94	77°	19·75	58°	7,332	7,405	7,370
,, 13	9 a.m.	Askordas		*22·90	66° ?	24·93	80°	19·65	59°	7,348	7,270	7,310
,, 13	10 a.m.	Samaiyar Bridge		*22·97	67° ?	24·92	83°	19·65	59°	7,438	7,517	7,480
,, 20	7.30 a.m.	,, ...		*22·72	60° ?	24·97	77°	19·72	58°			
,, 13	11 a.m.	Samaiyar		*22·85	69° ?	24·90	86°	19·65	60°	7,370	7,332	7,350
,, 19	8.45 p.m.	,, ...		22·89	69°	24·92	79°	19·73	61°			
,, 15	7.15 p.m.	Nagyr...		22·20	60°	24·81	79°	19·61	61°	7,837	7,746	7,790
,, 25	8 a.m.	,, ...		22·55	62°	24·93	77°	19·78	60°			
,, 26	5.30 p.m.	,, ...		22·47	72°	24·73	86°	19·68	62°			
,, 16	10 a.m.	Rope-bridge below Nagyr ...		*23·10	60° ?	24·90	84°	19·71	61°	7,055	7,130	7,090
,, 16	6 p.m.	Baltit Camp		22·33	59°	24·84	85°	19·58	62°	7,977	7,898	7,940
,, 18	12.45 p.m.	,, ...		22·32	68°	24·82	89°	19·60	61°			
,, 20	2.45 p.m.	Strawberry Camp		19·90	50°	24·94	89°	19·60	60°	11,242	11,188	11,210
,, 21	7 p.m.	,, ...		19·91	41°	24·91	76°	19·66	61°			
,, 21	8 a.m.	Samaiyar Glacier Plateau ...		17·86	43°	24·93	77°	19·73	59°	14,254	14,350	14,300
,, 24	9 a.m.	,, ,, ...		17·92	54°	24·97	80°	19·74	61°			

* Readings marked with an asterisk were taken with an aneroid recently corrected by comparison with the Mercurial Barometer.

Date.	Time.	Place.	Boiling Point. Fahr.	Barometer reduced to 32° Fahr.	Air Temperature. Fahr.	Gilgit.		Leh.		Altitude deduced by comparison with Gilgit (4,890 ft.).	Altitude deduced by comparison with Leh (11,508 ft.).	Mean Altitude.
						Barometer reduced to 32° Fahr.	Air Temperature. Fahr.	Barometer reduced to 32° Fahr.	Air Temperature. Fahr.			
June 21	9.45 a.m.	Samaiyar Glacier Upper Plateau		17·48	75°	24·98	83°	19·74	61°	15,262	15,006	15,130
,, 22	6 p.m.	Trough Camp		17·08	48°	24·88	85°	19·60	62°	15,557	15,358	15,460
,, 23	noon	Daranshi Saddle		15·59	32°	24·91	89°	19·69	62°	17,989	17,900	17,940
,, 27	6.30 p.m.	Rattallo Hopar...		21·25	63°	24·71	85°	19·64	62°			
,, 28	6 a.m.	,, ...		*21·42	60° ?	24·78	73°	19·69	60°	9,144	9,292	9,220
,, 28	6.30 a.m.	Holshal		*21·40	61° ?	24·78	74°	19·69	60°	9,064	9,232	9,150
,, 28	6.40 a.m.	Holshal Fort		*21·26	61° ?	24·79	74°	19·69	60°	9,261	9,416	9,340
,, 28	7 a.m.	Hopar Glacier rt. moraine edge		*21·51	56° ?	24·79	75°	19·69	61°	8,911	9,097	9,000
,, 28	8 a.m.	Foot of Barpu zigzags		*20·98	58° ?	24·79	77°	19·69	61°	9,650	9,784	9,720
July 1	6.45 a.m.	Barpu Camp		20·49	54°	no read	ings	19·63	63°		10,400	10,400
,, 1	12.45 p.m.	Mir		19·49	55°	no read	ings	19·62	65°			
,, 2	10.10 a.m.	,, ...		19·56	45°	24·95	84°	19·67	65°			
,, 2	2 p.m.	,, ...		19·69	53°	24·91	88°	19·57	66°	11,780	11,490	11,630
,, 3	1.10 p.m.	,, ...		19·56	45°	24·93	88°	19·62	67°			
,, 4	1 p.m.	Dasskaram Camp		18·01	52°	24·86	88°	19·68	67°			
,, 5	6 a.m.	,, ...		18·07	45°	24·90	73°	19·68	64°	13,956	13,973	13,960
,, 5	1 p.m.	Dasskaram Needle		15·90	65°	24·83	88°	19·65	67°	17,766	17,550	17,660
,, 6	6.15 p.m.	Paipering Maidan		19·97	62°	24·66	82°	19·60	67°	10,940	11,036	10,990
June 28	9 a.m.	Lower Rash Pass		*20·09	58° ?	24·79	80°	19·68	62°	10,882	10,986	10,980
July 7	noon	300 ft. below Upper Rash Pass		17·05	65°	24·74	88°	19·68	68°	15,648	15,629	15,630
June 28	10 a.m.	Huru		*21·45	70° ?	24·78	84°	19·68	63°	9,047	9,123	9,090
July 7	8 p.m.	Rash		19·17	58°	24·67	79°	19·62	67°	12,068	12,211	12,140
June 28	noon	First bridge over Hispar river		*21·78	75° ?	24·74	89°	19·64	64°	8,624	8,616	8,620
,, 28	4 p.m.	Second ,, ,, ...		*21·10	75° ?	24·68	91°	19·56	64°	9,441	9,348	9,400
,, 28	6 p.m.	Hispar		*20·44	68° ?	24·70	85°	19·56	64°			
,, 30	6 a.m.	,, ...		*20·49	60° ?	no read	ings	19·62	62°			
July 9	8 p.m.	,, ...		20·30	67°	24·57	79°	19·52	69°	10,295	10,348	10,320
,, 10	5 p.m.	,, ...		20·29	70°	24·58	85°	19·55	70°			
,, 11	9 p.m.	Chokutens...		19·33	55°	24·60	78°	19·50	70°	11,724	11,808	11,770
,, 12	4 p.m.	Gandar		18·49	59°	24·54	90°	19·51	71°	13,064	13,077	13,070

* Readings marked with an asterisk were taken with an aneroid recently corrected by comparison with the Mercurial Barometer.

Date.	Time.	Place.	Boiling Point. Fahr.	Barometer reduced to 32° Fahr.	Air Temperature. Fahr.	Gilgit. Barometer reduced to 32° Fahr.	Gilgit. Air Temperature. Fahr.	Leh. Barometer reduced to 32° Fahr.	Leh. Air Temperature. Fahr.	Altitude deduced by comparison with Gilgit (4,890 ft.).	Altitude deduced by comparison with Leh (11,508 ft.).	Mean Altitude.
July 13	6 p.m.	Haigutum		18·05	49°	24·66	82°	19·63	70°	13,766	13,985	13,880
" 14	11.30 a.m.	"		18·10	48°	24·75	88°	19·66	70°			
" 15	6.30 p.m.	Kanibasar Camp		17·78	43°	24·66	82°	19·51	70°	14,080	14,132	14,110
" 16	6.30 p.m.	Hispar Snowfield Camp... ...		17·06	41°	24·59	82°	19·49	69°	15,211	15,271	15,240
" 17	10.40 a.m.	" "		17·04	54°	24·64	83°	19·55	70°			
" 17	7.30 p.m.	" "		17·04	36°	24·63	79°	19·66	69°			
" 18	noon	Hispar Pass		15·80	64°	24·63	88°	19·55	70°	17,705	17,590	17,650
" 19	8 a.m.	Snow Lake Camp		16·44	30°	24·79	76°	19·62	67°	16,200	16,380	16,290
" 19	8 p.m.	Ogre's Camp		17·71	34°	24·59	79°	19·56	68°	14,134	14,335	14,230
" 20	7.45 a.m.	"		17·72	46°	24·75	76°	19·61	67°			
" 21	5.40 p.m.	Boggy Camp		18·14	54°	24·43	82°	19·36	69°	13,512	13,636	13,570
" 22	5.30 p.m.	"		18·04	50°	24·47	82°	19·47	69°			
" 23	9.15 a.m.	"		18·00	46°	24·62	83°	19·65	68°			
" 24	7.25 a.m.	Mango Brangsa		18·95	45°	24·72	76°	19·62	67°	12,514	12,696	12,600
" 25	8 a.m.	"		18·78	46°	24·80	76°	19·68	67°			
" 26	6.30 a.m.	Nambla Brangsa		19·46	46°	24·78	76°	19·58	66°	11,662	11,733	11,700
" 27	6.45 p.m.	Askole		20·47	67°	24·71	82°	19·50	69°	10,320	10,407	10,360
Sept. 5	6.45 p.m.	"		20·42	61°	24·73	69°	19·71	65°			
" 6	8.20 a.m.	"		20·46	57°	24·84	68°	19·69	63°			
July 31	11.30 a.m.	Edge of Biafo glacier		*20·61	80° ?	24·75	88°	19·66	70°	10,266	10,200	10,230
" 31	noon	Foot of Biafo glacier		*20·69	80° ?	24·75	88°	19·66	70°	10,154	10,088	10,120
" 31	6 p.m.	Korofon		20·45	71°	24·56	84°	19·54	69°	10,318	10,398	10,360
Aug. 1	6.15 a.m.	"		20·48	62°	24·71	75°	19·67	68°			
Sept. 5	noon	"		20·42	72°	24·79	80°	19·67	65°			
Aug. 1	9.30 a.m.	Laskam Pass		*18·86	70° ?	24·71	81°	19·67	69°	12,684	12,775	12,730
" 1	5.20 p.m.	Ghoresamakar...		20·16	74°	24·66	85°	19·53	70°	10,758	10,655	10,710
" 2	7 p.m.	Bardumal		19·91	69°	24·64	77°	19·51	69°	11,017	10,983	11,000
" 3	7 p.m.	Baltoro		19·50	66°	24·65	77°	19·52	69°	11,580	11,574	11,580
" 4	6.10 p.m.	"		19·61	69°	24·74	80°	19·58	70°			
Sept. 4	9 a.m.	"		19·68	59°	24·91	70°	19·74	64°			

* Readings marked with an asterisk were taken with an aneroid recently corrected by comparison with the Mercurial Barometer.

Date.		Time.	Place.		Boiling Point. Fahr.	Barometer reduced to 32° Fahr.	Air Temperature. Fahr.	Gilgit.		Leh.		Altitude deduced by comparison with Gilgit (4,890 ft.).	Altitude deduced by comparison with Leh (11,508 ft.).	Mean Altitude.
								Barometer reduced to 32° Fahr.	Air Temperature. Fahr.	Barometer reduced to 32° Fahr.	Air Temperature. Fahr.			
Aug.	5	6.30 p.m.	First Camp, Baltoro glacier	…		18·58	54°	24·78	80°	19·54	70°	13,059	12,968	13,010
,,	6	4.45 p.m.	Piale Camp	… … … …		17·90	57°	24·79	88°	19·56	71°	14,222	14,017	14,120
,,	7	4 p.m.	Storage Camp	… … … …		17·84	48°	24·72	88°	19·55	72°	14,225	14,196	14,210
,,	8	10 a.m.	,,	… … … …		17·82	49°	24·83	81°	19·65	70°			
,,	10	5.20 a.m.	Crystal Peak, table station	…		*15·89	45° ?	24·82	84°	19·68	68°	17,466	17,485	17,480
,,	10	6 a.m.	,,	breakfast-place..		*15·24	45° ?	24·86	71°	19·68	68°	18,498	18,642	18,600
,,	10	noon	,,	summit … …		14·83	45°	24·79	88°	19·63	70°	19,433	19,344	19,400
,,	10	3 p.m.	,,	foot of clear ice..		16·23	56°	24·75	88°	19·58	70°	16,968	16,828	16,900
,,	9	3.20 p.m.	Pool Camp	… … … …		17·38	51°	24·71	88°	19·56	71°			
,,	10	5.30 p.m.	,,	… … … …		17·41	55°	24·75	84°	19·58	70°	14,766	14,801	14,780
,,	11	8.40 a.m.	,,	… … … …		17·61	43°	24·81	77°	19·72	68°			
,,	11	7 p.m.	Fan Camp	… … … …		17·21	47°	24·71	77°	19·64	68°			
,,	12	5.30 p.m.	,,	… … … …		17·27	54°	24·68	84°	19·58	69°	15,062	15,139	15,100
,,	13	6.20 a.m.	,,	… … … …		17·27	46°	24·90	72°	19·63	68°			
,,	12	noon	Fan Pass …	… … … …		15·31	74°	24·71	88°	19·64	69°	18,847	18,676	18,750
,,	13	5.15 p.m.	Junction Camp	… … …		16·84	43°	24·74	84°	19·55	68°			
,,	15	10.10 a.m.	,,	… … …		16·87	43°	24·91	81°	19·59	67°			
,,	16	4.40 p.m.	,,	… … …		16·80	36°	24·87	88°	19·67	65°	15,893	15,846	15,870
,,	17	6 p.m.	,,	… … …		16·83	39°	24·82	80°	19·64	64°			
,,	29	1 p.m.	,,	… … …		16·67	59°	24·82	88°	19·64	66°			
,,	17		K. 2 (G. T. S. India 28,250 feet)				Measured by Theodolite from Junction Camp.							27,750
,,	17		Golden Throne†	… … …			Measured by Theodolite from Junction Camp.							23,600
,,	18	5.30 p.m.	Footstool Camp	… … …		16·26	39°	24·78	82°	19·59	64°			
,,	19	5.50 p.m.	,,	… … …		16·43	37°	24·70	80°	19·63	64°	16,351	16,500	16,430
,,	20	8.45 a.m.	,,	… … …		16·54	32°	24·78	77°	19·72	64°			
,,	27	7 p.m.	,,	… … …		16·21	37°	24·60	78°	19·45	68°			
,,	20	1.30 p.m.	Theodolite Station	… … …		16·22	67°	24·83	88°	19·66	65°	17,222	16,997	17,100
,,	21	9 a.m.	Top of first great serac	… …		15·62	55°	24·85	78°	19·73	64°	18,034	18,071	18,050
,,	21	5 p.m.	Serac Camp	… … … …		15·42	45°	24·66	84°	19·61	66°	18,112	18,257	18,200
,,	22	7.30 a.m.	,,	… … … …		15·45	38°	24·83	75°	19·74	64°			

* Readings marked with an asterisk were taken with an aneroid recently corrected by comparison with the Mercurial Barometer.

† See "Climbing in the Himalayas," pp. 486, 524.

Date.	Time.	Place.	Boiling Point. Fahr.	Barometer reduced to 32° Fahr.	Air Temperature. Fahr.	GILGIT.		LEH.		Altitude deduced by comparison with Gilgit (4,890 ft.).	Altitude deduced by comparison with Leh (11,506 ft.).	Mean Altitude.
						Barometer reduced to 32° Fahr.	Air Temperature. Fahr.	Barometer reduced to 32° Fahr.	Air Temperature. Fahr.			
Aug. 23	8.45 a.m.	Lower Plateau Camp		15·11	57°	no readings		19·71	66°		19,000	19,000
,, 24	3.45 p.m.	Upper Plateau Camp		14·53	60°	no readings		19·58	69°		19,970	20,000
,, 25	8.45 a.m.	Pioneer Peak, 1st point		14·12	39°	24·88	77°	19·72	67°	20,590	20,750	20,700
,, 25	11 a.m.	,, 2nd ,, ...		13·72	38°	24·81	84°	19·70	67°	21,348	21,350	21,350
,, 25	4.30 p.m.	,, ,, ,, ...		13·87	48°	24·67	88°	19·64	67°			
,, 25	3.30 p.m.	,, summit		13·27	54°	24·66	88°	19·64	67°	22,600	22,520	22,600
,, 29	6.45 p.m.	Goat's Delight Camp		17·20	40°	24·77	78°	19·58	65°	15,058	15,121	15,090
,, 30	6 p.m.	Hollow Camp		17·60	39°	24·76	81°	19·62	65°	14,427	14,539	14,480
Sept. 1	5.30 p.m.	Corner Camp		17·54	52°	24·74	78°	19·54	64°	14,469	14,536	14,500
,, 2	6.45 a.m.	,, ...		17·70	51°	24·85	64°	19·67	62°			
,, 4	7 p.m.	Dreary Camp		20·29	59°	24·82	69°	19·60	65°	10,672	10,590	10,680
,, 7	4.40 p.m.	Darso Brok		18·07	52°	24·72	81°	19·62	63°	13,770	13,846	13,810
,, 8	11 a.m.	Skoro La		15·90	36°	24·85	77°	19·68	62°	17,273	17,375	17,320
,, 8	6.30 p.m.	Skoro		22·33	59°	24·80	70°	19·65	61°	7,859	7,995	7,930
,, 9	11.20 a.m.	Shigar		22·51	72°	24·84	78°	19·69	61°	7,744	7,774	7,760
,, 10	4.50 p.m.	Skardo		22·74	74°	24·75	79°	19·57	61°	7,501	7,434	7,470
,, 11	3.30 p.m.	,, ...		22·55	71°	24·78	81°	19·57	62°			

Camps between Skardo and Leh; the altitudes were determined by a single barometric reading and by comparison with the corresponding Leh reading only:—

Thurgon	7,530 ft.	Tarkutti	8,640 ft.	Kharbu	11,990 ft.
Parkutta	7,870 ft.	Oldingthang	9,270 ft.	Nurla	9,520 ft.
Tolti	8,450 ft.	Kargil	9,160 ft.	Bazgo	11,050 ft.
Khurmang...	8,340 ft.	Shargol	10,600 ft.		

NOTES ON THE MAP.

NOTES ON THE MAP.

By W. Martin Conway.

An ideal physical map would be the representation in little, either in relief or on the flat, of a portion of the earth's surface, wherein every physical feature, large enough to be visible on the reduced scale, would be depicted accurately in form and position. Existing surveys of mountain regions do not enable this ideal to be approached even remotely, save in the case of certain portions of the Alps. Herr Imfeld's relief map of the Zermatt region is probably the best of its kind, and some parts of it—notably the Swiss slopes and ridges of the Matterhorn—are extraordinarily veracious and minute in detail. All the later work of the Swiss surveyors, as manifested in the sheets of the Siegfried map, approximates to the same admirable completeness, and immeasurably surpasses any other mountain survey in the world—exception being, perhaps, made in the case of the, as yet unpublished, map of the Mont Blanc district by Herr Imfeld himself. It is needless to say that my map does not belong in any respect to the same class as these triumphs of art and science combined.

Before mountains were studied, as the development of mountaineering, and that alone, has caused and enabled them to be studied, they were not regarded as physical features requiring to be truthfully mapped. Their importance as forming watersheds was obvious; so was the prominence of certain individual masses and peaks; but only the man, who either climbs mountains or looks at them with a climber's eyes, realises the individual importance of ridges, snow-faces, buttresses, and the like details. Surveyors before the time of mountaineering were satisfied when they had fixed with accuracy the position of the tops of the greater peaks and had indicated the trend of main ridges. A caterpillar-like diagram, with points for peaks here and there, sufficed to indicate all that geographers then cared to know. A modern physical geographer is otherwise inquisitive. He is not so much anxious for supreme accuracy in the position of peaks (though that is good if it can be had) as for information about the shape of the mountains themselves. He desires first and foremost to have the glaciation represented,—the limits between snow and rock, and the limits between snow and ice. As a rule where *névé* gives place to true glacier, moraines appear on the surface of the ice. Hence the marking of moraines is very important. It is also important that the catchment area of each glacier should be truthfully indicated. In fact the upper regions are of more importance than the lower, the only very material detail required to be known about the lower half of a glacier being the position of its snout. All glaciers are liable to be broken into ice-falls at parts of their course. The number and position of these ice-falls, and of much-crevassed portions which are not quite ice-falls, are the matter of next moment, and finally the form of the peaks themselves, with special reference to the way the snow lies upon them, the position of important couloirs, ice-slopes, and the like, and the nature of the ridges, and whether they present rock or snow arêtes. It is at least as advisable to observe the position of the lowest points of gaps and saddles between peaks as that of the summits of peaks—a fact by no means sufficiently remembered.

In the Himalayas there has been hardly any mountaineering, properly so called. The great mountains are still regarded much as Mont Blanc was regarded in the last century—a great white mass seen from a distance and looked upon as a unit instead of as a collection of individual peaks. Nanga Parbat and its attendant peaks cover a larger area than the whole Mont Blanc range, but they are looked upon as a single mountain, and no one takes any interest in the satellites. There has therefore never arisen any demand for a record of the detailed form of this or any other great Himalayan mountain, or of the shape of the snow-mantle that covers it.

The Great Trigonometrical Survey of India is one of the most remarkable survey undertakings ever attempted in the world. If so vast an area was to be mapped with even approximate truthfulness, it was above all things essential that the position of points should be determined with perfect accuracy. Such accuracy seems to have been throughout attained, as far as human powers reach. The peaks, whose positions are determined, do, in every important case, occupy the positions indicated for them; but there, as far as the Karakorams are concerned, the accuracy ends. The caterpillar convention is employed to fill up the gaps, doubtless often to the no small injury of the surveyor's work. In saying this I am not criticising the Survey; the work that it undertook has been well done, and does not require to be done over again; but to fix the position of peaks is merely to lay a foundation upon which it will take a long series of years to build. The map herewith issued is an attempt to supply a very small portion of the superstructure.

The area covered by my map is included in the sheets, 27A N.E., 44A N.W., and 44A S.W., of the Indian Atlas. From those sheets a mountain student cannot learn much, for the very good reason that they were not constructed with a view to his enlightenment. No attempt has been made in them to depict the glaciation of the country; and only the position of glacier troughs is indicated, the direction of ridges, and the situation of peaks. There is nothing to show whether a mountain is snow-covered or rocky, whether its ridges are narrow or broad, whether its faces are steep or gentle. The anatomy of the ranges is not given. The map is merely a map of valley bottoms. In no case are the snow reservoirs shown. No ice-falls are marked, no crevassed areas indicated, no moraines dotted in. The European mountain lover will inevitably believe that all this implies censure on my part, whereas nothing of the kind is implied.

The portion of the mountain region under consideration was surveyed, as far as its details are concerned, by Colonel Godwin-Austen, F.R.S., in the years 1860 and 1861.* That was at a time when the craft of climbing was in process of invention in the Alps, and long before any notion of it had penetrated to other parts of the world. Nowadays when a range of mountains has to be surveyed by any Govern-

* Royal Geographical Society's Journal, 1864, p. 19.

ment—the Caucasus, for instance, or the New Zealand Alps—it is clearly perceived that the glaciation of the hills is of first importance, and that the form of peaks must be shown, but in 1861 no such idea prevailed. Colonel Godwin-Austen was only asked to sketch in the lower parts of the glaciers and the position of the chief ridges, and that he accomplished perfectly well, as far as his route permitted him to see. He attempted no more. He only looked up the Biafo glacier; hence his sketch survey of that could not be more than an impression. All the upper part of that glacier is totally different in fact from its representation on his map. He only saw the Hispar glacier from the Nushik pass, so that he could do no more than sketch in his idea of the peaks beyond it, as seen from a single point of view. He only ascended the lower half of the Baltoro glacier; the upper part of it was always hidden from him, and he could not see more at any time than the point of the summit of K. 2 appearing above Crystal Ridge. There have, therefore, to be removed from his map the whole basin of the Hispar glacier, all the Biafo glacier except its bottom twelve miles, and all the Baltoro glacier above my Hollow Camp. These areas were practically, and, by Colonel Godwin-Austen's own admission, unsurveyed, and my survey of them was a survey of unexplored country. It is only from Mango Brangsa on the Biafo glacier down to its foot and up to Hollow Camp on the Baltoro glacier that both Colonel Godwin-Austen and I covered the same ground with our actual surveys. Of the approximately 2,500 square miles included in my map, not more than 500 square miles were surveyably visible from points on Colonel Godwin-Austen's recorded route. The other parts of the country surveyed by me (except Bagrot) are either blank on the Indian Atlas sheets or filled in with imaginary detail. Let it, however, be clearly understood that Colonel Godwin-Austen surveyed a large area of mountain country in the Karakorams which I never saw at all, or saw only as he saw the Hispar basin, the upper Biafo, or the upper Baltoro.

The map with which persons, knowing in mountain matters, will naturally compare mine is Adams Reilly's map of the Valpelline, Valtournanche, and the southern valleys of Monte Rosa. The comparison, however, is not just. Reilly's map was the work of two seasons, and includes an area of about 500 miles. Mine was made in eighty-eight days, in the midst of a mass of other work, and covers approximately five times that area. There was, moreover, a quantity of material in existence which Reilly could use, the like of which was not available for me.

Turning now to my own map, I will briefly indicate its scope, and the conditions under which it was made.

My journey was not primarily intended to be a surveying expedition, but a mountaineering expedition. It was our intention to explore as large a portion of the glacial area as we could cover in a season, and to ascend as many peaks as possible, but not to halt on our way for the sake of multiplying ascents or of investigating details. We wished to see much rather than minutely. Moreover, I intended to take many photographs, to make all the scientific collections I could, and to write every day a full account of the day's doings. These things were the first charge on our time. The map was secondary to them, and intended so to be.

Knowing this beforehand, I had to consider what aims I should set before myself in map-making. Obviously, from a mountaineer's point of view, the glaciation was of first importance. It was clear that the existing survey gave no idea of the actual glaciation, it being impossible for glaciers to exist without snow-fields, and there are no snow-fields marked upon it. It was not important to fix with great accuracy the position of numerous summits, but the succession and character of the peaks was required, and especially their nature and the general form of their snow mantles. It was no part of my plan to halt anywhere for the sake of getting second sights. If a peak hid itself, that bit of the map had to be omitted or merely sketched in.

Some parts of the map were originally drawn on a scale of two miles to an inch; others on the scale of 1¼ inches to a mile. Every detail of rock faces, ridges, ice-falls, and the like that time permitted to be sketched in on the spot was recorded. Over a thousand photographs were taken for the purpose of further elaboration of detail in the redrawing at home. As works of art the photographs were not very good; but they were invaluable for topographical purposes. The scale was too large for convenient working on the small plane-table. If I had the work to do again I should adopt the scale of four miles to an inch, and trust more to photographs for details than I did.

The surveying instruments employed were a 3-inch transit theodolite and a small plane-table. It was my intention to carry on a continuous triangulation, but the cloudy weather rendered this impossible, and the various portions had afterwards to be connected by help of the points determined by the Indian Survey.

On my return to England I spent nearly four months in drawing out the whole map afresh, on the scale of one inch to a mile, and colouring it as in the published copy. My manuscript map is deposited with the Royal Geographical Society. This was afterwards re-drawn on half the scale by Mr. Scharbau with great dexterity, but many of the details had to be omitted, and others were not understood by a draughtsman, wonderfully painstaking and accomplished though he was, unfamiliar with snowy regions and the phenomena they present. The published map, therefore, does not indicate the position of ice-falls, snow-plateaus, and crevassed portions of glaciers so truthfully as my own manuscript, in which the detail was all intentional and, as far as my skill extended, truthful.

Coming now to the published map, it is perhaps well that the quality of the various parts should be stated in order. It was, as I have stated, drawn on the march and inked in nightly in the tent. It practically represents the employment of the time secured by the difference between our pace and that of the slow-going coolies.

The head of the Bagrot valley was the first portion surveyed, and occupied nineteen days. The mass of Chiring Chish is accurate in detail, and so is most of the Gargo basin, but, owing to the continuous bad weather, it was never possible to connect these two portions accurately together. I never saw the upper basin of the Bagrot glacier, and the great snow-field there depicted is really an unsurveyed area.

The survey was recommenced near Gulmet, and the portion between Gulmet and Hispar was done in twenty-seven days. Here again bad weather constantly interfered with my work and rendered it incomplete. The snowy area of the Budlas peaks was only sketched in from a great distance, a bit one day, a bit another day. The Samaiyar valley is fairly accurate except as regards the top area of *névé* which I never saw clear of clouds. The same statement applies to the upper level of the Bualtar glacier, and of the Shallihuru and Samaiyar Bar glaciers, the south-east basin of which is doubtless incorrectly sketched in. The Guarbun glacier was never seen, but only the upper portions of the ridges surrounding it, and the same is true of the *névé* of the Lak glacier, which was always buried in clouds and storm.

The portion of the map between Hispar and the Hispar pass was made in eight days. The snow-fields of all the side-glacers are of course merely sketched in, but the whole of the south ridge, from Haigutum to the pass, is, I believe, very accurately rendered. The upper portions of the Kanibasar glacier and of the great nameless side-glaciers to the east are almost entirely conjectural, as only the ridges were in sight and the ends of the glaciers between them. Clouds were seldom lifted off this remarkable region, which can only be surveyed in detail by ascending each glacier to its head.

The Biafo glacier was surveyed in eight days. I only once saw its upper levels, which were far too intricate for me even to venture on sketching them in from so brief an inspection. I need only say that there are no "undulating snow-fields" in this region at all, but only almost flat *névé*

—the flattest I ever saw—with ridges and peaks rising steeply out of it. The peaks around the Latok glacier were always hidden by clouds, and all I could see was the ends of the glaciers dividing or descending from them.

The survey of the Baltoro glacier took twenty-six days. The portion below Masherbrum is merely a correction of the G.T.S. survey, with the addition of a quantity of details taken from photographs and sketches. The upper part is a new survey altogether, but here again the *névé* basins of many of the side-glaciers were never visible, and their form could only be even approximately inferred from that of the ridges surrounding them.

It is, of course, the *névé* basins that are really the most important parts of any mountain region; but they can only be surveyed by penetrating to them. Whatever we could see is represented; and we saw all that in the time and weather was possible to be seen. To survey the Baltoro glacier as it should be surveyed, without even then attempting to approach the excellence of the Swiss map, would take the whole of two seasons' work. Some day, no doubt, this will be done. In the meantime the work here given to the public is as accurate as time and means permitted, and is put forth without apology, though with full consciousness of its unavoidable limitations.

NOTES ON MR. W. M. CONWAY'S COLLECTION OF ROCK SPECIMENS FROM THE KARAKORAM-HIMALAYAS.

NOTES ON MR. W. M. CONWAY'S COLLECTION OF ROCK SPECIMENS FROM THE KARAKORAM-HIMALAYAS.

By Prof. T. G. Bonney, D.Sc., F.R.S., and Miss C. A. Raisin, B.Sc.

During his journey in the Karakoram-Himalayas, Mr. W. M. Conway collected more than three hundred specimens of rocks and minerals, which, however, were generally rather small. These he entrusted to us for examination at University College, London. Thin slices have been prepared of those specimens which promised to be the more interesting. Of the rest the mineral composition was verified in cases of doubt by examining pulverised fragments under the microscope. Except in the case of rocks of more than ordinary interest, we have deemed it generally needless to enter into the details of these investigations, and have restricted ourselves to their results. It will facilitate description to group roughly the specimens under the usual heads, commencing with the most basic of the crystalline rocks. The numbers in square brackets are those placed on the specimens by Mr. Conway.

Serpentine, &c.

[8], from *débris* below a slope at the village of Mapnun, Burzil pass, dark green, slightly mottled, with small glittering crystals of bastite. Under the microscope the ground-mass of the slice exhibits a closely felted structure of very minute somewhat fibrous minerals, the polarisation tints being blues rather of the third order. In parts are granules and short belonites or elongated prisms, which appear mostly augite, their mode of occurrence suggesting that they are fragmental constituents of larger grains of this mineral. The grains of bastite are irregular in outline. Iron oxide is also present; it is generally decomposed, but in some cases appears to be chromite. The original rock was probably an enstatite-peridotite with some augite. The rock evidently has been much crushed, and is traversed by veins of chrysotile and other minerals. These have been subsequently disturbed. It closely resembles a type of serpentine not uncommon in the Alps.

With the above-named rock we may put a talc schist [191], from the right moraine of the Samaiyar Bar glacier, as probably having had a similar origin, though now completely altered and too crushed for microscopic examination.*

Diorites, &c.

Several rocks which are almost hornblendites lead up to the more normal diorites. One of the former [23], from a fallen block, western side of Astor valley above Dashkin, is a dark green, rather friable rock, which consists chiefly of hornblende, mostly in porphyritic crystals about three-quarters of an inch long. More than one variety of this mineral appears on microscopic examination, one blue-green (for rays along the c axis), yellower green (for direction at right angles), the other of larger crystals strongly dichroic (b dark bronze-green, c similar but slightly darker, a straw-colour). In the latter, enclosures probably hematite are rather frequent, which apparently lie in the pinacoidal planes.† We find also some plagioclase felspar, a little pseudobrookite, rutile, and pyrite. The rock has suffered from pressure, which has caused locally the formation of a chlorite and possibly of some secondary felspar.

The specimen [25] from the same locality seems to be a schistose form of a similar rock. It consists mainly of a blackish, glittering, fibrous hornblende, and thus is very dark green in colour. Its surfaces are somewhat slickensided, with films of green copper ore. A few elongated grains of clear felspar or quartz appear on microscopic examination, but the slice consists almost entirely of hornblende in rather elongated prisms, with a very definite orientation. This is markedly dichroic, changing through bluish-green (c axis) to grass-green (b axis), or almost colourless (a axis); it contains occasionally small crystals of rutile, rather impure, arranged along the cleavage planes. A system of parallel planes extends continuously across the crystals of the slice whatever their orientation, roughly making angles of 70° and 110° with the foliation. Even in one grain of (?) quartz, lines of enclosures seem to continue the direction of these planes. The rock is now a hornblende schist, but it was probably produced by pressure from one closely allied to a pyroxenite.

Specimens [44] from a fallen block near Bunji Bridge, right bank of Indus, and [139] from the Bagrot valley‡ are also almost hornblendites. Less normal in character are [193], from 300 feet below the Upper Rash pass, *in situ*, which includes a fair amount of felspar, although the rock is still clearly porphyritic, and [14], from near Mykiel, Burzil valley (*in situ*), which is only slightly porphyritic. A small crushed specimen of hornblende schist [143] from gorge below Gwech, Nomal valley, § higher up than [142], may be derived from a rock similar to the original form of [25]. It now consists of normal actinolite, perhaps in itself an indication of pressure,|| some brown mica, plagioclase felspar, and a little iron oxide.

* T. G. Bonney, *Geol. Mag.*, 1890, p. 540.

† These might be similar to the enclosures in schillerised pyroxenes described by Prof. Judd, which, however, consist of mixtures of limonite and other oxides. See Q. J. G. S., 1885, vol. xli. pp. 379, 381, 384, &c.

‡ Right bank of Bagrot valley below Bulchi is strewn with blocks like 139, 136, 137. —W. M. C.

§ The strike is 2½° N. of E.S.E., dip 50° northerly. The strike below Gwech near [142] was 8° N. of S.E., dip 85° north-easterly. The general strike of the valley to Chalt was 2½° N. of E.S.E., dip usually nearly vertical. Between Chalt and bridge and across the river the strike was 9½° N. of E.S.E., dip 85° northerly.

Strike and dip, in the case of the crystalline rocks, may be regarded as referring to the dominant structure, which would often be a master-joint.

|| See T. G. Bonney, Q. J. G. S., 1893, vol. xlix. p. 101.

Next come the more normal diorites. First of these is a small fragment of an extremely coarse diorite [16] from fallen rock on right slope of Burzil valley, at the Mykiel gates, close to exit into Astor valley, consisting of irregularly formed hornblende crystals, quite one inch in length (in which one or two small crystals of biotite are enclosed), and of a decomposed felspar of saussuritic aspect with some hornblende interspersed. A small piece of a similar but somewhat less coarse variety, [52], is common in *débris* shortly above Sinakar, Bagrot, but these specimens are ill suited for microscopic examination.

Of the diorites which exhibit more definite ophitic structure, [136], Bagrot valley, may be taken as typical. This is a moderately coarse rock composed of dark green hornblende and yellowish-white felspar. Under the microscope the felspathic constituent itself appears to be composite and to contain many thin blades or often scales of hornblende imbedded in what is apparently a reconstituted felspar, in which occasionally dusty aggregates, (? epidote) are present. The large hornblendes vary from dark brown, with patches of bright green or very pale yellow (rays parallel to *c* axis), to dark brownish-green (*b* axis), to light raw sienna-brown (*a* axis). Some altered biotite is present in the slice (varying from pale bright green or very pale green to cream colour) and also a small amount of a clear mineral like quartz. The rock is a diorite, but probably the constituent minerals are mainly of secondary origin.

In a similar diorite [137] from the same locality, consisting of plagioclase felspar, hornblende, brown mica, and epidote, the hornblende tends to aggregate in black patches with smaller felspar, apparently partly replaced by epidote (porphyro-glomeratic structure). The proportion of felspar and hornblende varies slightly in different examples, but two similar specimens occur in [140], which exhibits a fairly marked orientation of its constituents, and [142], both from the lower part of Nomal valley above Gilgit.* The parallelism in [12], from a fallen block on the right bank of Burzil valley near Das, and in [50], about one hour up the Bagrot valley on the right bank, some 500 feet above the stream, is somewhat slight (strike near the latter 5° W. of N., dip 45° easterly), but more definite in [22], the normal rock of the west side of valley below Astor, and apparently also of the east side. The next specimen [93], from block on an old moraine at Gargo, Bagrot, is a foliated rock consisting apparently of a white saussuritic mineral and of dark green hornblende in rather fibrous prisms, with a somewhat streaky and patchy arrangement. Microscopic examination shows the ground-mass to be a mosaic of grains, mostly rather small (about ·004 inch in diameter), of quartz and felspar (some being plagioclase), with a number of elongated crystals of dark green, strongly dichroic hornblende (some measuring ·2 inch in length, ·008 inch in breadth), disposed in rather ill-defined layers. The form of the crystals is generally irregular, occasionally they include grains of quartz or felspar, and often appear more like a fascicular aggregate of small actinolite than one perfectly uniform crystal. Grains of magnetite occur, and a few of (?) zoisite, which, however, may be in a vein. The structure of the rock suggests pressure-modification—it is now a foliated epidiorite, and probably was once a gabbro.

A specimen from the gorge at Ramghat, near Bunji [42], is a slightly banded diorite or a hornblende schist. The microscope shows the constituents to be rather granular, and to be a dark green hornblende, probably secondary, and a somewhat decomposed plagioclase felspar, perhaps labradorite, with apparently some epidote not very pure. The rock is probably igneous, but does not show marked signs of crushing. [288], from the Indus

* Further up the strike is E., dip various. Strike usually rather more parallel with valley. Dips various from 45° to vertical.

valley, between Parkutta and Tolti,* is a similar rock, but without the parallelism. [13], from a fallen block on the right bank of Burzil valley near Das, is a rather compact variety showing joint surfaces. [59], from half-way between Sinakar and Datuchi (strike 7½° N. of E.N.E., dip 75° south-easterly), Bagrot valley,† is a compact black diorite with green prismatic hornblende, felspar, mica, iron oxide of more than one form, some being limonite and probably pseudobrookite.

The rock [246] from Angle peak (at angle of Godwin-Austen and Baltoro glaciers) consists of green hornblende, felspar, brown mica, with zircon and some small clear prisms, possibly beryl; it is probably a diorite or syenite. [101], from *débris* covering the left side of Gargo glacier,‡ contains little felspar but much epidote in the ground-mass. It is rather compact, but perhaps exhibits signs of pressure-modification. [141], from a cliff close to river, Nomal valley, above Nomal, is a similar rock, but the specimen is mostly vein of quartz, (?) calcite, and epidote.

[61], common in the left moraine of Bagrot glacier, is typical of a series of specimens. It is a compact greenish-grey rock, veined with epidote, and containing idiomorphic crystals of dark green hornblende, rather stumpy, from a quarter to half an inch in diameter. Under the microscope the ground-mass consists of a small bladed variety of a pale clear green hornblende intercrystallised with a glass-clear mineral (often plagioclase), which sometimes predominates in spots. The large porphyritic hornblende crystals are generally similar to those just mentioned, but in places prove to be somewhat composite in structure, consisting of aggregated flakes of a dark green hornblende, with some chlorite, epidote, and perhaps felspar. We think that probably the ground-mass of this rock has been entirely reconstituted, and that even the larger crystals in their present form may be of secondary origin. It is a proterobase or uralite diabase. Very similar specimens are—[139], from the right bank of the Bagrot valley below Bulchi, containing finely disseminated epidote in the ground-mass; [166], along left bank of Nagyr valley,§ in which the porphyritic crystals are smaller; they are slightly more crowded in [121], from left moraine of Burchi glacier,‖ somewhat crushed. [165], from left bank of Nagyr valley,§ is irregularly porphyritic, and in it very minute silvery mica has formed. This appears more developed in [53], which is common in *débris* shortly above Sinakar. In [175], from a thin vein on top of Rash ridge, right above Barpu Camp, is a small node, or possibly an enclosed fragment. Two very rotten and iron-stained specimens [47, 46], from a fluviatile deposit "near right bank (of Indus river), just beyond Bunji Bridge," probably were diorite, and apparently (in [47] atleast) contained large hornblende crystals. [5], from a fallen block near the camping-ground, Gurai, "on north side of Tragbal pass," is a compact pale green rock, probably a diabase, the specimen apparently being bounded by surfaces of flattened rhomboidal jointing.

Next come some schistose rocks, or schists, which are almost certainly diorites or

* This, alternating with granite, is the general rock in the valley between these places.—W. M. C.

† This is the general rock of the valley here. It occurs again further up near Gordi waterfall, behind Chira, and continues up both sides of the valley. Just below the waterfall the rock of the lower part of the valley on east side for half a mile seems to join the main mass of the mountain.—W. M. C. Other strikes recorded are 7½° E. of E.N.E., dip vertical (near seam of 54); and 10° S. of E., dip 80° northerly, near Gordi waterfall; and N., dip 40° easterly, just below the waterfall, for half a mile on east side in lower part of the valley.

‡ This specimen and 100 are characteristic of the *débris*.—W. M. C.

§ 165, 166 are common all along the left bank. They also are strewn along all the left side of the Bualtar glacier, and seem to come from the Crown of Dirran.—W. M. C.

‖ 120, 121, 122 are rocks common in this moraine.—W. M. C.

dolerites, pressure-modified. [133], *in situ* at left foot of Bagrot glacier, a rather slaty schist of greyish-green colour with somewhat silvery lustre, seems to be composed mainly of a greenish hornblende with small streaky patches of yellowish epidote. Under the microscope the rock has a somewhat minute, slightly undulate foliation, consisting of small actinolitic crystals of hornblende associated with a minutely granular aggregate of fairly transparent felspar, or closely allied minerals, with a carbonate. There is a fair amount of iron oxide, probably magnetite, in small granules arranged in slightly wavy streaks. More or less regular grains, probably replacing partly crushed crystals, now chiefly epidote, and certain elongated patches, consisting mainly of calcite, occur. While the structure of the rock at present is not easily described, there can hardly be any doubt that it was formed by the pulverisation of a doleritic rock, followed by partial recrystallisation. Rocks almost identical with it occur among the "grüner schiefer" of the Alps. [116], "from foot of Burchi mass by right side of Gargo glacier" (strike 5° S. of E., dip 60° southerly), is similar, also with a few small nests of epidote; and [73], from a moraine on the left of Gargo glacier, between Gargo and foot of glacier, without the epidote clusters, shows part of the mould of a cubic mineral, probably pyrite, between which and the matrix of the rock quartz and felspar have been locally deposited. [77], from the same moraine, includes part of a vein of quartz with some copper staining. [94], from the Gargo glacier, near the left bank, is a large specimen of a similar rock with some epidote, and crowded with cubes of pyrite. [58], from above Sinakar,* mainly consists of actinolite, like that in [5], and of fine-grained felspar. It is a green rock, probably a modified diorite, which has been crushed but not rendered fissile or foliated.

[54], occurring across the Bagrot valley above Sinakar,† is a compact greenish, waxy-looking rock, not unlike a felstone, made heavy by abundant pyrite, and weathering brown on the outside. Examination of a thin slice shows the matrix to consist chiefly of epidote and of a transparent mineral in somewhat elongated grains or ill-defined prisms, which give rather low polarisation tints and occasionally exhibit twinning; probably this is a secondary felspar. With these occur crystalline grains of (?) colourless augite, nests of more platy or fibrous colourless hornblende, and crystals of pyrite passing to limonite often bordered by translucent blood-red hematite. The rock seems to be entirely constituted of secondary minerals, but probably it was originally a rather felspathic diabase.

Certain rocks approach fine-grained micaceous diorites in character. [169], from near and south of Hopar, contains larger flakes of greenish-black mica in a compact pale green matrix. [218], a pressure-modified rock from the Green Parri, near Askole, is rich in hornblende of a rather actinolitic type; it also contains a good deal of biotite and a little of a whitish felspar. [194], from the upper part of Rash ridge,‡ includes much felspar (often clear plagioclase), brown mica, some (?) quartz, hornblende, and some slightly rounded small prisms of apatite. The rock is a mica-diorite, probably modified by pressure. A calcareous pisolitic material on one surface is apparently a tufaceous deposit. [130], from the rocks at the foot of Dar valley, Bagrot, much crushed, containing patches of limonite, consists mainly of a dark green mica, and includes a fair amount of rutile. It may be possibly an altered mica trap. [119], from near Burchi glacier, is greatly modified by pressure, a laminated pale green rock, and consists mostly of green mica with some actinolite. [242*b*], from the ascent to White Fan pass,§ Baltoro glacier, consisting of

* This appears to be associated with specimens 54 to 57.—W. M. C.

† 54–57. Patches and big seam across the valley. The rock disintegrates very much and colours big fans below.—W. M. C.

‡ This rock forms all the upper part of the ridge (towards eastern end).—W. M. C.

§ There were dark masses of 242 and white bands of 243.—W. M. C.

felspar, quartz, brown mica, hornblende, with a little (?) zoisite and zircon, seems more nearly related to the mica-syenites.

Granite and Gneiss.

We begin with granites of normal type, moderately coarse-grained, the mica (variable in character and amount) being generally biotite, bronzed in [4], from a fallen block near the camping-ground, Gurai, north side of Tragbal pass; black in the others. It is small and shows slight orientation in [43], from near Bunji Bridge, on the left bank of the Indus. The rock [224], from *in situ* above Baltoro Camp, north of the valley, is porphyritic, showing a Carlsbad twin of orthoclase. Only a little mica is present in this specimen, and in the following: [278] and [279], from *in situ* all along the left bank of the lower portion of Baltoro glacier; [11], from *in situ* a little way up the Burzil valley; [167], from medial moraine of Bualtar glacier; [209], forming the bulk of right moraine of Biafo glacier (the needle-peaks seem to be made of this); [225], material of the grey moraine right side of Baltoro glacier; [233], from *in situ* at the angle where Piale joins Baltoro glacier; [207], found at Snow Lake Camp, Biafo glacier (somewhat gneissoid; strike 10° N. of E., dip 60° northerly); [308], from left bank of Baltoro glacier. The constituents of some of these show a very slight orientation. [210], from eastern angle of foot of Latok glacier, is rich in biotite. This granite forms the bulk of the *débris* on the Biafo glacier to this point. [202], from *in situ* at Kanibasar Camp,* is more felspathic, containing some microcline, and also hornblende as well as biotite. [159], from *in situ* in the Samaiyar valley, two hundred yards west of Strawberry Camp, is finer-grained and possibly slightly pressure-modified.

Next come many micaceous gneisses, not markedly banded, clearly crushed, probably resulting from the crushing of normal granites. The original rock in [37], from 50 feet below Hatu Pir (strike 10° N. of E., dip 33° southerly), and in [200], from Hispar valley, near Haigutum (strike 2½° N. of E.S.E., dip about vertical), was porphyritic, for these are now augen-gneisses, the latter being the more micaceous. The remaining gneisses, like the granites, vary somewhat in the amount of mica, which is only small in [36], from 200 feet below Hatu Pir (strike 10° S. of E., dip 33° southerly), and not very much in [195], a representative specimen of the fallen stuff on right bank of Hispar valley. This rock is almost a syenite, with mica as the second constituent, but it apparently contains some quartz, and is evidently crushed. [172], near Barpu Camp, on Rash ridge, is similar, consisting of felspar, quartz, and biotite, with some zircon.

The amount of mica increases in the series: [35], from just north of Doian Fort (strike 10° N. of N.E., dip 50° south-easterly); [38], from gorge below Hatu Pir; [31], from rock *in situ*, a short distance north of Trubyling, Astor valley (strike 5° E. of N.E., dip 30° south-easterly); [154], at Shaiyar fort gate (*roches moutonnées*) (strike 10° S. of E., dip 20° southerly); [217], at Nambla Brangsa Camp, Biafo glacier,† [206], from behind Hispar Snowfield Camp, on the north bank of the Hispar glacier (strike E.S.E., dip 60° northerly); [21], from boulder in the *débris* through which the side stream flows on which Astor is built; the amount of mica culminating in [287], from Skoro La (a much crushed specimen), and in [208], from behind Ogre's Camp, Biafo glacier (strike 5° N. of S.E., dip 80° south-westerly), in which biotite is abundant in fairly large flakes. This rock is probably a

* Most of right moraine of Hispar glacier above junction with Kanibasar glacier consists of 202 with a good deal of 203.—W. M. C.

† From table station 59, the strikes seen were on left bank of Biafo glacier, 10° E. of N.E., dip 80° north-westerly; on right bank, strike N.E., dip 75° north-westerly.—W. M. C.

crushed granite, like [210], only rather richer in mica. [48], from a fluviatile deposit, near right bank of Indus, just beyond Bunji Bridge, is a gneissoid rock, probably pressure-modified, somewhat rotten, consisting chiefly of felspar and abundant dark green hornblende and mica. In the powder the felspar is clear, being sometimes plagioclase; brownish mica, green hornblende, probably rutile, sometimes decomposed, and (?) anatase are present. Two gneisses are markedly coloured by red-stained quartz and felspar, associated in [30], from a slope on the west side of the Astor valley, near Dashkin, with biotite, and in [19], from a fallen block on the left bank of the Astor valley, opposite Mykiel gates (a rather crushed specimen), with much silvery mica.

A small specimen [32] from rock *in situ* north of [31], north of Trubyling (strike 2½° N. of N.N.E., dip 45° easterly), is probably a banded gneiss, for it shows parts of a micaceous and a quartziferous band crumpled up together. [201], common among fallen blocks on Haigutum slopes, Hispar glacier, is a micaceous gneiss closely laminated, showing in one part light grey and dark bands. It consists of black and colourless mica, quartz, and felspar, with a fair quantity of rutile and occasionally zircon. The felspar under the microscope has the water-clear look, and the enclosures of needles, &c., which often characterise rocks of an ancient series. The specimen is traversed by a quartz-felspar vein formed along a fault plane. The banded structure has been crumpled by subsequent pressure. [173], from near Barpu Camp, Rash ridge,* is somewhat similar, perhaps richer in biotite; and [160], from ice-worn rocks "on left bank of icefall, Samaiyar glacier" (strike E.S.E., dip 55° southerly),† is also of the same type, but includes a few small nests (¼ inch by $\frac{1}{16}$ inch) roughly oblong, richer in black mica. Among the microscopic constituents small zircons sometimes occur. [56], from the Bagrot valley above Sinakar, is a weather-worn specimen in which, however, felspar, some white mica, a pale green actinolitic hornblende, and fairly abundant rutile, sometimes in well-defined prisms, can be distinguished on microscopic examination. [102], from *in situ* on a hill overlooking left bank of Gargo glacier above the icefall (strike 2½° N. of E.N.E., dip 75° southerly), appears to be compounded of a minutely granular mixture of quartz and felspar, with a fair amount of pale green mica, specks of limonite probably replacing pyrite, and some very minute opacite. The rock, not improbably once a gneiss, has been greatly crushed, showing small crumplings and strain slip-cleavage.

[186], from Dasskaram Needle (strike 5° S. of S.E., dip cir. 75° south-westerly), appears to be a somewhat ill-preserved pressure-modified gneiss with brown-stained felspar, and mica colourless and brown. This leads up to a series of specimens, which are all fine-grained gneisses pressure-modified, although their small-granular structure is not due to crushing. They resemble certain speckled rocks found in the district near Blair Athol, which Dr. H. Hicks has happily designated "pepper and salt" gneisses. The next rocks also somewhat resemble this group. [180], from near Mir Camp (strike 7½° S. of E.S.E., dip 80° southerly), which consists of felspar, often a clear secondary variety, of brown and of white mica, the latter sometimes containing brown clots, as if it might be derived from the brown by separation of the iron. The rock is fine-grained, crushed, and may have been originally a mica-diorite. [214], from the right moraine of the Biafo glacier,‡ in addition to plagioclase felspar, quartz, and brown mica, contains a pale greenish mica, and a mineral,

* Rash ridge consists of rocks 170-174. The strikes are from 10° S. of S.E. to 2½° N. of S.S.E., dips various. Near Barpu Camp, dips 30-60° southerly.—W. M. C.

† Higher up the strike is 10° S. of S.E., dip 80° south-westerly.

‡ The rocks 213-216 are common in this moraine below the glacier coming in above Mango Brangsa, but not higher up.—W. M. C.

rather dirty with enclosures. It is probably garnet, but has more signs of cleavage than is usual. [29], from the roadside between Harcho and Dashkin,* Astor valley, is a fine-grained black and white rock in laminæ, which have a thin, streaky, drawn-out shape. It is rendered granular, almost sandy, by crushing, and weathers brown. The rock is a gneiss with some similarity to the "pepper and salt" type. The chief minerals are brown mica, felspar, much of which under the microscope contains clear enclosures and has the appearance of the felspar in old gneisses, while some is plagioclase with rather small extinction angle. There is little or no quartz. The accessories are a reddish garnet, fairly abundant zircon, crystals of rutile, and others of a decomposition product, probably that said by Rosenbusch to be identical with leucoxene.†

The following specimens include some more typical: In [222], from the eastern angle of the junction of the Punmah and Baltoro valleys (strike 5° N. of S.E., dip 70° south-westerly), black mica is scattered rather uniformly through the specimen. On microscopic examination the rock is seen to consist mainly of a mosaic of quartz and felspar (some plagioclase), much brown mica having definite orientation, with small zircons, some needles probably kyanite, one or two grains possibly andalusite, and (?) epidote. The specimen recalls some Alpine mica schists in the neighbourhood of intrusive granite. [237*a*], from the north of Baltoro glacier, near Storage Camp,‡ has a similar texture, so as to give a gritty feel to the weathered edges, but is rather evenly laminated. [283], "from western angle of junction of Punmah and Baltoro valleys," is a brown-stained specimen from a banded gneiss, with quartz, felspar, and dark mica; and similarly brown-stained is a small squeezed micaceous specimen [161*b*], from east face of north ridge of Trough Saddle § (strike 2½° E. of N.N.E., dip vertical). The remaining examples of this "pepper and salt" type of gneiss are perhaps more fine in texture and close in grain as in the flake [168], from near and south of Hispar,‖ and in [163], from Samaiyar valley, between foot of glacier and mouth of valley (strike 5° S. of S.E., dip nearly vertical).¶ In [153], on north bank of Hunza river, a quarter of a mile east of Tashot Bridge (strike 10° S. of E., dip 85° southerly),** the minute mica causes a filmy and sheeny surface. [149], from two-thirds of the way from Gulmet to Tashot, below the watch-tower, is also a slightly banded variety (strike 7½° N. of E.N.E., dip 60° southerly). [309], from the left bank of Baltoro glacier, a fine crushed gneissoid

* The general rock by the roadside here consists of rock like 28, 29. The strikes recorded in the Astor valley are: Two miles below Astor, E., dip 45°; close to river, 15° W. of N., dip 30° easterly; at first galleries, 10° W. of N., dip 30° easterly; gorge near Parri, 10° E. of N., dip vertical; two miles below Parri, 10° E. of N., dip vertical; before reaching Harcho nala, 10° W. of N., dip 75° easterly. Below Lipscomb, beds much contorted on both sides of valley.

† "Micr. Petrogr. of Rock-forming Min." (J. P. Iddings), p. 148.

‡ Some of this rock is included in the granite 233, strike 2½° N. of S.S.E., dip 10° westerly. Other strikes recorded from north of Baltoro glacier are 2½° S. of E.S.E., dip 45° northerly; and 12° S. of N.E., dip 50° northerly (at junction of Piale and Baltoro glaciers). —W. M. C.

§ Found all down the left moraine of Samaiyar glacier and all along Mir moraine.—W. M. C.

‖ Yarpun mass and Hunnuns, strikes 5° S. of S.E., dip 30° south-westerly. Mouth of Sepultar nala, strike 5° S. of S.E., dip 30°. Rash Chish, opposite end of Barpu glacier, strike 7½° S. of E.S.E., dip 50° southerly.

¶ About half-way to glacier foot the strike is 12½° S. of E.S.E., dip 85° south-westerly. A foot of glacier, right side, strike is 7° S. of S.E., dip vertical.

** Strike near Hunza rope-bridge is along the valley, but dip is only about 10° southerly, with much contortion. On south side of Hunza river, opposite the Chashi nala, strike is 5° N. of E., dip 45° southerly. In Nagyr valley, half-way between Nagyr and Samaiyar, the strike is 12½° S. of E.S.E., dip 75° northerly.

rock, includes in the powdered material felspar, brown mica, iron oxide, and a tourmaline with perhaps some quartz.

Somewhat akin to the above, but slightly coarser, is [280], from a medial moraine by Bruce's Camp, Baltoro glacier, and considerably more coarse [199], from above second plane-table station on Shukurri (strike 12° N. of S.E., dip 75° south-westerly).* Here may be mentioned also several specimens which have some characteristics in common with this group. [220], from a higher part of Laskam ridge, is a compact dark purplish-brown rock bounded by even divisional surfaces. A thin slice on examination exhibits a mosaic of quartz with some felspar, brown mica, some white mica, hardly any free iron oxide, possibly a little zircon. The rock appears to be a fine-grained mica gneiss or mica schist, the rather peculiar structure of which is possibly due to reconstitution after crushing. Except that the specimen is not banded, it recalls one of the rocks near Muchalls, Aberdeenshire.† [238*a*], from the north bank of Baltoro glacier, Pool Camp (strike 15° S. of E., dip 65° south-westerly), appears similar. A dark, slightly purplish-grey compact rock with micaceous surfaces, not unlike a quartzose band from a crushed micaceous gneiss. The powder exhibits brown mica and some white, felspar, quartz, (?) some pyrite, and frequent minute included specks of opacite or (?) pyrite. Among the powdered constituents of [240], from the south flanks of Crystal Peak, are felspar, mica, some quartz, and many grains and aggregate spots of iron oxide, usually hematite. The rock is almost a slate in aspect, but it includes the constituents of a gneiss, and is probably due to the crushing of such a rock. [241], also from south side of Crystal Peak, consists chiefly of scales of lead-coloured mica and of small granules of felspar, and exhibits a corrugated foliation. It is a crushed mica gneiss. [203], from right moraine of Hispar glacier above junction with Kanibasar glacier,‡ is an exceedingly fine-grained, dark, rather slaty-looking gneissoid rock, which proves to consist chiefly of rich brown mica and felspar, both containing opacite. There is some possibility that it might be a case of contact metamorphism.

Several gneissose rocks are streaked with thin filmy layers of a green mica (or chlorite). [20], from a boulder in the *débris* traversed by the side stream on which Astor is built, is distinctly crushed, and contains silvery mica as well as the pale green mica. Microscopic examination shows the felspar to be partly a fresh-looking variety, not twinned, and partly plagioclase somewhat decomposed. The rock may have been originally a mica-syenite. In [227], from moraine on left of Baltoro glacier, the chief minerals are a rather dusty felspar and green mica, possibly a little hornblende, and some epidote, sometimes in well-crystallised prisms. The rock is poor in quartz, and approaches a mica-syenite or diorite. [213], common in right moraine of Biafo glacier below the glacier coming in above Mango Brangsa, but not higher up. This consists of similar minerals to those in [20], but with some quartz, and may be a gneiss formed from a granitoid rock by crushing. [62], from top of Bari Rung ridge, above right bank of Bagrot glacier, includes similar felspar, possibly of two varieties, green and colourless mica, and grains (sometimes pyramidal) of magnetite.

We may place next a group of garnet-bearing rocks. One granite [192], from half-way up Rash ridge, south side, contains large red impure garnets, three-quarters of an inch in diameter, intercrystallised with irregular, still larger patches of felspar, in a fine-grained ground-mass, consisting of much black mica, some quartz and felspar, with zircon. Some of the grains fracturing like quartz, with polarisation tints of a clear

* This rock is the common material of the moraine of the Hispar glacier.—W. M. C.

† Q. J. G. S., 1886, vol. xlii.; Proc., pp. 97, 98; Pres. Addr., T. G. Bonney.

‡ Most of moraine consists of 202, with a good deal of 203.—W. M. C.

bluish-grey, seem to have an unusually high refractive index for that mineral. The rock also contains small (one-quarter of an inch) porphyritic crystals of very clear felspar. The garnets include all the minerals of the ground-mass, but the mica shows signs of alteration, being rather green. The rock is gneissoid in structure, and has been probably produced by the crushing of a porphyritic granite. Another porphyritic rock [27], from *in situ* near Parri, between Astor and Dashkin, and common in the *débris* all along the valley, is yet more crushed, forming an "augen" gneiss, the "eyes" (sometimes three-quarters of an inch by one-quarter of an inch) being a glassy-looking orthoclase, showing pearly cleavage faces, and occasionally a Carlsbad twin. The pinkish garnets (one-twelfth of an inch to one-quarter of an inch) present sometimes the appearance of "eyes," or may be imbedded within those of large felspar, and the latter mineral under the microscope proves to be rich in very clear, acicular, oblong, or other regular-shaped microliths. The matrix consists of similar felspar, brown mica, with small prisms, possibly kyanite. [170], from near Barpu Camp, is a gneiss, but finer grained, with very much brown mica and some green, with felspar, some quartz, minute garnet, and rutile. This, doubtless, results from the crushing of a less coarse porphyritic granite. [171], from the same locality, is a dark, speckled, compact rock, with scattered red garnets. It might be a fine-grained kinzigite, or a garnet-diorite with a very faint foliation. Microscopic examination proves it to consist of quartz, abundant clear plagioclase, brown mica, and garnet, the last being irregular in form and interspersed with grains of other minerals. The rock retains traces of a fragmental structure, and possibly might be an altered grit, but the more probable origin is a crushed and partially reconstituted crystalline rock.

The next rocks are more or less characteristic examples of granulites. [28], one of the normal rocks by the roadside in the Astor valley, between Harcho and Dashkin, is a fine-grained, laminated gneiss, containing felspar, rutile, a little biotite, some (?) pseudobrookite, with numerous minute garnets, sometimes so small and close as to give a pinkish tinge to layers and parts of the rock. It is rich in quartz, especially in some laminæ, and is a true granulite (Leptynite). [151], from a side nala leading from Tashot to Fakkar (strike 2½° S. of E.S.E., dip 85° southerly, but varying in a few yards), is a brown-stained, friable rock of somewhat similar character, containing brown mica, felspar, (?) quartz, a fair amount of rutile, occasionally zircon, and a mineral which probably is pseudobrookite. The rock is akin to a granulite, though garnets seem to be wanting.

[314], from near Askole, either a quartzite or a quartz vein crushed, with a thin, silvery surface layer, chiefly an aggregate of a fibrous mineral like sillimanite. The specimen includes garnets (pyrope), in some of which brown mica seems to form as a surface film. The rock is crushed, and nests of the brown mica at places resemble in form crushed garnets, like those of Mysore.* The mica possibly may partly replace garnet, or still more probably may develop around the garnet crystals as the halo of "kelyphite" described by Diller.† The next are mineral rather than rock specimens, but as containing garnet, may be mentioned here. [284], from "western angle at junction of Punmah and Baltoro valleys," is a rather flattened garnet, about three-quarters of an inch across, with silvery mica wrapping around it, and is very probably from a mica schist. In [315], from near Askole, red garnets (one-quarter of an inch), often changed to limonite, are imbedded in an aggregate of (?) mica and chlorite (probably clinochlore).

* See T. G. Bonney, Q. J. G. S., 1888, vol. xliv. p. 651, and Pl. 15.

† Bull. 38. U. S. Geol. Surv., 1887, p. 15. See Rosenbusch, "Micr. Physiogr. of Rock-Making Min." (J. P. Iddings), p. 132.

Felstones.

The collection contains few of the more compact acid igneous rocks. Normal specimens are almost absent, but a series from the vicinity of the Golden Throne may be best noticed here. The rocks [291] [292] [293] from the moraine starting from the west foot of the mountain are compact, but show a schistose structure with slightly micaceous or talcose aspect, indicative of crushing. They are particoloured, a grey, varying from slightly to markedly greenish, being streaked, spotted, and blotched with a dull indian red, small white specks showing in some of the patches. The texture of the lighter part under the microscope is speckled, or somewhat fibrous, with indications of minute aggregate polarisation, this being most conspicuous when it makes an angle of 45° with he vibration planes of the crossed nicols. The mineral very closely resembles the so-called sericite of some porphyroids. Here and there are grains of quartz, decomposed and sometimes broken felspar crystals, and some dark reddish, flaky patches. The dark macroscopic spots contain corroded grains of quartz, decomposed or partly corroded felspar crystals, and the same dark red, flaky minerals in a crypto- to micro-crystalline matrix. In one rounded lump, at first sight very like a pebble, some grains of crystalline calcite are enclosed. The smaller patches, though varying in detail, present a general resemblance, and there can be little doubt that they are fragments of a devitrified acid igneous rock. In the absence of definite characters it is difficult to speak positively as to the nature of the matrix, but most probably it was once a volcanic glass, which has since undergone micro-mineralogical change, mainly in consequence of pressure.* Though the red patches occasionally look very like pebbles, it is more probable that they are due to a flow brecciation. If we are right in our inferences, these rocks of the Golden Throne indicate an outpouring of acid lavas prior to the mountain making.

Very similar specimens from the same locality are [294], of the same silvery white and red colours; [295], with red fragments or veins, crushed, imbedded in the pale green matrix; and [296], more red-stained. [297], probably also igneous, includes rather lenticular fragments of vesicular aspect, perhaps indicative of flow brecciation.

[231], from the left half of the Baltoro glacer, is a fragment of an indian-red rock of rather slaty structure, with whitish or greyish spots, the largest full one-quarter of an inch in diameter. Under the microscope the red matrix shows a somewhat fissile structure, and looks as if composed of devitrified glass in a minutely fragmental condition, but it is so much stained with hematite that a definite conclusion is impossible. But the unstained fragments large and small, while they closely resemble the two types of material described in the above group of specimens, differ one from another in several minor points. Hence the rock is either a tuff, subsequently modified by pressure (which seems more probable), or a very exceptional case of flow brecciation similarly treated. A duplicate smaller specimen [231] occurs.

[254], from Golden Throne, or its glacier, is also of an indian-red colour, but has smaller enclosures, which, in most cases, may be only altered crystals of felspar. Probably it is a crushed felstone. A specimen [147] from water-rolled *débris* at Gulmet bears considerable general resemblance to this. It is probably a felsite or porphyrite of a dark claret-red colour, with small porphyritic crystals of white felspar. Small enclosures effervesce briskly, and so are probably calcium carbonate. The presence of this material in the body of the rock is indicated by HCl in most of the above specimens, sometimes in small, sometimes in large amount. Probably it is usually an infiltration product.

* As has happened in many porphyroids. T. G. Bonney, Proc. Geol. Assoc., vol. ix., 1885, pp. 250-258.

Hornblende and Chlorite Schists.

The next group consists of rocks with a definite foliation, whatever may be its cause. [49], from the west side, south end of Bagrot valley (strike 2½° N. of E.N.E., dip 55° northerly), shows under the microscope felspar and clear green prismatic hornblende, and is a strong, compact hornblende schist, like that of the Lizard, or of Sark, though finer grained and with more indications of crushing. Another hornblende schist [282] from *parri* at west angle of junction of Punmah and Baltoro valleys, is less markedly crushed. [104], [105], from rock in couloir of Emerald Peak (strike 7½° N. of E.N.E., dip 30° southerly), are found on microscopic examination to consist of brown mica, much of a hydrous green mica, or more probably a chlorite, possibly some hornblende, grains of epidote, a felspar which is clear and most likely secondary, and a carbonate resembling calcite. The hardness of the specimens is less than 3, so chlorite rock may be the most appropriate name. [18], from rock *in situ* right bank of Astor river, just outside Mykiel gates, is another chlorite rock, evidently crushed. It shows when powdered felspar, a little epidote, some rutile, and a good deal of a green mineral having one fairly definite cleavage and a slight tendency to a fibrous structure. The mineral extinguishes perpendicular to the edge of the most perfect cleavage, and is probably an hexagonal chlorite. [91], from the left moraine of the Gargo glacier below the icefall, consists of small green chlorite and mica, with a vein including pyrite and calcite.

Epidote Schist.

[51], common in Bagrot valley *débris*, is a crystalline rock moderately foliated, and not markedly fissile, consisting largely of epidote, evidently interbanded with more hornblendic layers. Microscopic examination proves the most abundant mineral to be epidote; with this occur hornblende, quartz, calcite, and a fairly strong brown garnet, with a little of a nearly colourless mineral, possibly augite. The rock is an epidosite, but is probably interbanded with hornblende schist as at the Lizard.

Piedmontite Schist.

We come next to specimens of piedmontite schist, all from Gargo glacier. [87], from the left bank or moraine, shows in a rich purple compact matrix a number of dull white spots, rather fragmental in aspect. These exhibit a slight orientation, and traces of divisional surfaces are perceptible, cutting this at an angle of rather over 35°. Quartz, white mica, and piedmontite, the first being the most, the second the least abundant, and some felspar are the principal minerals shown in the slide. The quartz contains enclosures, generally minute, but variable in size, occasionally with bubbles. The piedmontite occurs in more or less clustered grains or irregular short prisms. With ordinary transmitted light the mineral exhibits a great variety of tints, from rather dull pale orange or straw colour to a rich purplish pink or strong orange red, inclining sometimes to a burnt-sienna, sometimes to a more purple hue. On testing for dichroism we find in sections parallel to the orthodiagonal, the colour changes from pale pink (parallel to $\mathfrak{b}$ axis) to rich pink ($\mathfrak{c}$ axis, as stated by Lévy *), and in sections more or less transverse from pale yellow to burnt-sienna, and in some sections from deep amber ($\mathfrak{a}$ axis *) to a rich pink or slightly orange purple. The grains are apt to be irregular in external form, and seldom exhibit a perfect crystal outline; generally also they have a rather dusty look, as if they contained numerous small enclosures. We find also one or two grains of a mineral rather irregular in outline,

* "Les Minéraux des Roches," p. 184.

which has two cleavages crossing at a large angle, and exhibits not very high polarisation tints. It is probably monoclinic or triclinic, and a secondary product. In parts of the slide, crystalline granules of iron oxide (? hematite) are fairly abundant, and exhibit a somewhat streaky arrangement. Under the microscope the white spots of the rock consist almost wholly of crystalline quartz, and have a somewhat brecciated aspect. This suggests that the specimen may be from a vein, but the rest of the rock in structure more resembles a schist. There seem to be some slight indications of mechanical disturbance, but if this has occurred it must have been followed by a very considerable recrystallisation. [80], from a small boulder on the south bank of a stream flowing from the east through the maidan of Gargo. This appears to be a rather compact and hard schist, which evidently contains a fair amount of white mica in very small scales, and is rather rich in piedmontite. At the first glance the slide exhibits a large number of crystals of piedmontite, similar to those already described, together with small garnets and two micas, one colourless, the other brown, in little films, all scattered in a fairly glass-clear ground-mass; one or two grains of iron oxide and possibly rutile occur. The crystals generally have a foliated arrangement, and are somewhat irregularly grouped, comparatively free lacunæ occurring here and there. The garnets are clear, and contain a few enclosures (? cavities); they usually occur in well-formed dodecahedra, and are about ·002 inch in diameter. This is seldom and very slightly exceeded, but much smaller specimens are not rare. The white mica is less abundant where the garnets are common and has a tendency to be in larger crystals and group itself round the lacunæ. With crossed nicols the greater part of the ground-mass exhibits a rather minute mosaic structure, and is probably, at least to a considerable extent, secondary felspar. The larger interspaces prove to be in some cases aggregated granules of quartz, in others an almost water-clear felspar, cleavage planes and occasional twinning being perceptible. The outline of the felspar is very irregular, and it is associated sometimes with granules like those above mentioned, as though it had been partly replaced by them. There can be no doubt that the piedmontite, the garnet, and possibly some of the white mica, are of secondary origin. It is even doubtful whether all the larger grains of felspar and quartz are intact, for some contain more microliths than might have been anticipated. Calcite occurs locally in patches; in one place also a slightly granular mineral, giving bright tints with crossed nicols. The rock is now a piedmontite schist, but it is difficult to suggest what its original condition may have been —not impossibly it was once a fairly coarse-grained gneissoid or granitoid rock. Another specimen [86] brought from *débris* on the left half of the Gargo glacier bears some resemblance to the preceding one, but it is less micaceous and paler in colour; also it contains a vein of quartz with some minute calcite. Even on microscopic examination the distinctions for the most part are only varietal, but broken felspars of considerable size are rather more conspicuous in the specimen, and the rock generally affords very marked indications of fracture and reconstitution. The garnets run to about half the size of those in the last case. [90], found with specimens [86–89, 91, 92], from left side and moraine of Gargo glacier below icefall, has a general resemblance to [80], but has a slightly more slabby character. An examination of a small piece of the powdered rock fully confirms the macroscopic appearance.

These rocks have been compared with a specimen of the piedmontite schist of Japan, presented to one of us by the kindness of Professor Koto. This contains the characteristic mineral about as abundantly and as well developed as the Gargo specimens, but has more iron-glance (?), and more white mica, which sometimes seems to be slightly tinted by the manganese. The rock also is more definitely foliated.

Mica Schists.

[150], from Hunza valley, between Gulmet and Tashot,* is a dark, lead-coloured schist containing garnets. The latter on microscopic examination are found to be a pale reddish colour, sometimes fairly regular in outer form, cracked, granular in structure, and often containing a fair amount of dusky enclosures. These have a somewhat dendritic grouping; the angles which the tufts make one with another are such as to suggest relations with the process of crystal building. Also tubes or fibrous cracks are present, arranged generally at right angles to the faces of the garnet. Rather irregular crystalline grains of yellowish staurolite with many enclosures occur; also irregular grains of magnetite, and numerous little patchy flakes of brown mica. These are all set in a crystalline matrix, consisting of white mica and apparently granular quartz, with usually a considerable quantity of opacite, probably graphite, a few small tourmalines strongly dichroic, changing from a light to a brownish or dull greenish tint, and some small rutiles. The rock bears a very close resemblance to some of the black garnet-schists of the Alps.†

[316], from near Askole, apparently water-worn, is a somewhat silvery dark mica schist, containing black garnets. The dark colour of the rock seems due to very minute opacite contained within the colourless mica and in felspar, and to crystals probably of iron oxide (? magnetite). The black garnets seem to owe their colour to a similar substance. The powder also contains rather abundant prisms of a dull greenish, smoky tourmaline which contains some opacite.

[239], from the south flanks of Crystal Peak, a squeezed and crumpled schist with much dark, lead-coloured biotite, is probably due to crushing of a similar mica schist without garnets. [65], from a moraine on Bagrot glacier, is a dark crushed schist with silvery surfaces. The powder includes some felspar, white mica, some green mica or chlorite, possibly hornblende, iron oxide, much of which forms a staining and admixture in grains visible in the hand specimen. [178], from Mir Camp, is a pale green schist with small patches of a dark green mica (?). The powder includes clear felspar, some quartz, white and brown mica, (?) garnet, a green mica or chlorite partly decomposed, some rutile, and iron oxide, probably magnetite, which forms a surface deposit of minute granules.

Schists Containing a Conspicuous Secondary Mica.

[157], from a fallen block on left bank of Samaiyar valley, near glacier, a grey, streaky rock with numerous minute scales of mica, the general appearance suggesting "pseudostromatism."‡ Under the microscope the rock chiefly consists of a minutely granular clear mineral, which may be partly quartz, partly felspar, with numerous scales of white mica, up to about ·06 inch long, but generally smaller. In this ground-mass irregular flakes of brown mica are scattered, sometimes like drifting clouds, sometimes with grains of pyrite and iron oxide (limonite). The proportion of biotite varies in different parts of the slide. There are also prisms of dirty (?) hornblende. The rock evidently owes its present structure to very severe crushing, and the larger biotites, as more fully explained below, have been subsequently formed.

[188], from Dasskaram Needle, is a pale grey, closely laminated silvery schist, markedly calcareous (effervescing with HCl), including minute dark grains. It contains numerous

* Many fragments of this rock were lying along the bottom and slopes of the valley. Multitudes of garnets were found a little higher up the valley.

† T. G. Bonney, Q. J. G. S., 1893, vol. xlix. p. 105, &c.

‡ See Q. J. G. S., 1886. Proc., p. 65.

crystals of dark mica, as much as a quarter of an inch across, their outline being clearly marked and sometimes hexagonal. These commonly traverse the foliation planes at a high angle, and are uuusually thick. Thus the edges, which project from a weathered silvery surface, have the form of oblong prisms, and somewhat resemble, as the colour varies from a very dark green to almost black, crystals of hornblende. Under the microscope the ground-mass exhibits a foliated and slightly banded structure, and apparently consists partly of small grains, some seemingly calcite; others, rather irregularly formed, partly free from enclosures, of a water-clear mineral, giving somewhat low polarisation tints and with a kind of zoned structure, are probably secondary felspars, which may retain traces of an original nucleus. The ground-mass contains also mica, the larger crystals of which exhibit a curious and interesting structure. The mineral is generally of a light brown colour, becoming of a greener tint near to the outside. The former part is fairly dichroic, varying from a light, slightly greenish-brown to a fairly rich warm brown; but the greener parts are paler and not dichroic. The crystals are usually somewhat irregular in outline, but the cleavage is fairly good. In parts of the slide the mica appears in numerous small patches, mixed up with the ground-mass. These in some places seem to coalesce by a gradual replacement of portions of the ground-mass, so as to form ultimately a kind of setting for the grains which remain. In other parts, however, though a considerable portion of the ground-mass persists, the characteristic cleavage of the mica can be readily detected,* its pleochroism being wanting, though straight extinction is quite discernible. In these cases we have as it were the ghost of the mica, but commonly, as the mineral becomes more and more characteristic and pleochroic, the constituents of the ground-mass correspondingly disappear, until at last only few of them remain. In these, however, the original orientation is still preserved. Towards the edge of some of the grains the white mica, chlorite, &c., of the ground-mass seem as it were to pierce the brown mica. It is quite clear that the formation of this mineral is subsequent to the production of the cleavage foliation.† The manner of its occurrence suggests very strongly that its composition differs but slightly from that of an average sample of the ground-mass.

We are indebted to Mr. P. Williams for the following analysis, made in Prof. Ramsay's laboratory in University College. It should be mentioned that as only a very small amount of the mineral could be spared for analysis, he was placed under considerable difficulties, and found it necessary to compute the alkaline constituent as potash. It must also be remarked that the crystals often are not quite free from particles of the ground-mass.

SiO_2	30·3
Al_2O_3	24·7
Fe_2O_3	7·7
CaO	7·3
MgO	8·6
K_2O	14·0
Loss	9·6
	102·2

* The cleavage locally is so strongly marked that at first sight one almost anticipates a twinning. The cleavage seems to be present, but very little of the mica. In a well-known fairy tale the "Cheshire cat" vanished all but the grin; here, however, we have the grin in advance of the cat.

† See T. G. Bonney, Q. J. G. S., 1893, vol. xlix. pp. 104-113, Fig. 1, p. 107.

The above analysis corresponds generally with that of a hydrous mica, but it has a higher percentage of potash than is usual. It differs from biotite, which the mineral most resembles, in the larger percentage of alumina (in which it comes nearer to muscovite) and in the amount of lime. So far as it can be classified, it appears to be a hydrous biotite, with a considerable part of the magnesia replaced by lime.

[187], also from Dasskaram Needle, is a similar specimen, but the ground-mass consists mainly of quartz and (?) felspar with less calcite. We find also white mica, brown mica, epidote, some in longish prisms, iron oxide, and rutile, and long prisms granular colourless, with an oblique extinction and bright polarisation colours. The secondary biotite, mostly pale brown, includes all the above minerals.

Sericite Schists, &c.

The following may be described as mica schists, or allied rocks extremely crushed.

[67], from a mass in Kamar nala (strike at angle between Kamar and Bagrot nalas, 2½° N. of E.S.E., dip vertical), is one of the more quartzose, less micaceous, and is rich in pyrite. [83], from right moraine of Gargo glacier below the icefall, is a crushed sericite schist, crowded with pyrite or very possibly marcasite. The powder shows under the microscope some clear felspar and quartz, and fibrous patches, often greatly crushed, probably a mixture of chalcedonic quartz and felspar with fine silvery mica. [82], from the same moraine, is a small pebble of a felspathic rock (pressure-modified), consisting of perhaps more than one variety of felspar, a little greenish mica, and some grains of pyrite. [181], from a gully one hour from Mir (strike 12½° S. of E.S.E., dip 85° south-westerly), mainly a quartzose band, partly brown-stained, with micaceous surfaces, is probably from a similar rock.

The next three very pale green silvery specimens come from a mass at foot of Dar valley, Bagrot, and are all clearly pressure schists. [127] is a crushed mica schist. The powder consists largely of secondary felspar, with much fine silvery mica (little or no quartz), and includes a geniculate twin of rutile, and probably a little minute acicular tremolite. [126] is similar, containing a few small red patches apparently stained with iron oxide. The only mineral at all distinct in the powder of [128], which is clearly a pressure schist, is a very minute colourless mica. [107] and [108], from close by Sulphur Camp, Emerald Peak, seem to be rock generally similar to the last, but are much stained, the latter being coated with sulphur. [97], from the foot of Birchwood Hill, on the left of Gargo glacier (strike 2½° S. of E.S.E., dip (?) 40° northerly),* is a fissile actinolitic schist, the result, perhaps, of crushing a not very basic hornblende-schist or a hornblende-gneiss.

Schists partly Calcareous.

[183], from a gully more than an hour and a quarter beyond Mir, is a crushed silvery schist with small dark prisms of a fibrous greenish (?) hornblende. The powder contains much felspar, much of a carbonate, a colourless mica, some dull green mica, a pale tourmaline and fairly abundant rutile, sometimes connected with an opaque iron oxide, probably hematite. The rock is a somewhat calcareous mica schist. [176], forming the bulk of the rocks on the left and central parts of Samaiyar Bar glacier, is a crushed silvery mica schist. The powder contains mainly aggregates of clear felspar and (?) quartz, with

* Strike half-way from glacier foot to Gargo, left bank, 5° S. of E., dip 60° northerly; on top of peak E.S.E. of Gargo, 7½° S. of E.S.E., dip 80° northerly.

a carbonate, probably dolomite. [117], from rock *in situ*, 500 feet above Burchi Camp, is a squeezed whitish rock with green micaceous laminæ. The powder contains calcite, brownish biotite, greenish and silvery mica, felspar, and prisms of hornblende (?). The carbonate is abundant, so the rock may be termed either a calcitic-gneiss or an impure calc-mica schist much crushed. A crushed greenish schist [71] comes from the left moraine of Gargo glacier between foot of glacier and Gargo. The constituents shown under the microscope are felspar, sometimes of aggregated character, a fair amount of a carbonate, probably dolomite, a green mica, some pale green actinolitic hornblende, rutile in large amount in small prisms, sometimes geniculate, and perhaps a little epidote. The rock might be called a mica-dolomite schist, but a precise name is hardly possible.

[64], from the left side of Bagrot glacier, is a whitish or pale fawn-coloured crystalline limestone, with imbedded cubical pyrite and a silvery fibrous mineral. The powder consists largely of dolomite, or calcite, of pyrite, some decomposed, of quartz, of a (?) pyroxene, and a mineral fibrous in habit with a slight bluish tinge, probably sillimanite or (?) kyanite. Hence the rock is probably an impure calcareous quartzose sillimanite schist. [238*b*], found *in situ* near White Fan, Baltoro glacier, consists of alternating thicker and thinner white layers of subtranslucent quartz and of calcite, and is an evenly laminated calcitic quartz-schist.

Crystalline Limestones.

In this group [221] from the east side of Laskam ridge, *in situ* (strike as of 219, 11° S. of S.E.), is rather coarsely crystalline, slightly crumbling. It contains besides calcite a fair amount of colourless mica, and also some faintly-tinted crystals of (?) phlogopite. [193], from *in situ*, 300 feet below the Upper Rash pass, is more coherent, and contains specks of pyrite. [239], from the south flanks of Crystal Peak, is moderately coarse, and is crossed by two thin irregular bands, which are almost black from disseminated opacite. [244], from the ascent to White Fan pass,* has partly a grey-greenish tinge. [155], from a fallen block on left bank of valley near Samaiyar glacier, is fairly coarse with irregular grey spots, and with a few filmy patches of green copper ore.

Several specimens are more or less pressure-modified. [152] comes from one of two or three beds, (?) twenty feet thick, cutting across the gully leading up from Tashot to Fakkar.† This shows under the microscope the ordinary structure of a moderately coarse-grained marble, which has undergone a little pressure. There are one or two grains of a colourless silicate, possibly malacolite, and sundry granules of limonite, apparently replacing pyrite. [237*b*], from north bank of Baltoro glacier, near Storage Camp (strike 10° N. of E., dip 85° southerly, much contorted), is a finely-laminated white and grey, somewhat friable limestone, much resembling some of the crushed crystalline limestones of the Alps, such as, for example, occur near Saas Fee. The slice consists mainly of small granular interlocking crystals of calcite, but is crossed by thin laminæ of larger calcite with well-marked rhombohedral cleavage. Grains of malacolite occur sparsely, colourless and brightly polarising, generally rather small, but one larger crystal tails off at the ends as if from the effects of pressure. A few flakes of white mica also lie partly along the lamination, and granules of a black mineral (? graphite) variable in size and with a streaky arrangement. The rock is allied to hemithrene, and no doubt was originally more coarsely crystalline.

* This seemed to belong to a green mass, with thin seams of noble serpentine 245, all in mass west of side glacier, high up, above col.—W. M. C.

† Hereabouts are multitudes of garnets.

[241], from south side of Crystal Peak,* is also a crushed crystalline limestone. The powdered material consists mainly of calcite, but includes a mineral, probably a hornblende.

[145], from close to [144], which was between Chalt and bridge. The powder consists chiefly of fairly large crystalline calcite, often with oscillatory twinning, also flakes of white mica, one of brown mica, some felspar, a very distinct crystal of zircon, a slender prism (? apatite), and occasionally a red-brown grain (? pseudobrookite). The rock is pale grey and white, finely laminated, and of a crumbling granular texture. It is apparently a saccharoidal crystalline limestone, which has been very much crushed by a force acting at right angles to the planes of deposition. Rocks similar to this, and with a like history, occur in the neighbourhood of Saas Fee.†

The following specimens effervesce slowly or slightly in cold HCl, and are probably dolomite. [219], from half-way up to Laskam pass (strike 11° S. of S.E., dip 40° south-westerly), is saccharoidal, rather crumbling, fairly coarsely crystalline. [240], from south flanks of Crystal Peak, is less coarse, a rather dull white limestone (hardness 4), showing only very faint traces of lamination. [243], from ascent to White Fan pass, is crystalline dolomite, the crystals being small and probably including some calcite. [257], from Golden Throne and from left bank of Throne glacier, is a compact dull, greasy-looking rock, light grey in colour.‡ [259], from moraine from west foot of Golden Throne, is also compact, mostly whitish, in part a dark grey, somewhat veined. On one side is a small patch of aggregated minute copper pyrites. [318], from near Askole, is a white crystalline dolomite; s.g. 2·85.

SEDIMENTARY ROCKS.

LIMESTONES, &c.

The ordinary sedimentary rocks come next; first the limestones. [2], from Jhelam valley, below Baramula, is a dark blackish-grey, compact limestone, rendered rather streaky in aspect by roughly parallel, thin, whitish veins. [298], from Baltoro glacier, is a dark, slate-coloured limestone. [299], from the same glacier, is a greyish limestone, almost completely covered with a cream-coloured tufaceous deposit, pisolitic on one surface. [285], from dripping spring at west angle of junction of Punmah and Baltoro valleys. Evidently a fragment of a similar deposit.

[120], common in left moraine of Burchi glacier. The powder exhibits fragments of crystals, probably dolomite or calcite, colourless and some green mica, some felspar, and (?) tourmaline. Minute green specks and scattered pyrite are visible in the rock. This is a pale cream or fawn colour, weathering brown, is compact, and somewhat resembles a clayey felstone, but as it effervesces with HCl is most probably an argillaceous limestone. A finely laminated, rather compact pale brownish rock from Gusherbrum, [277c], proves to be an impure limestone. [300], from Golden Throne, a pale reddish rock, looking rather like a felstone; the matrix, however, has a hardness less than 4, and effervesces briskly, so it is probably a compact impure limestone containing small fragments of quartz and felspar. With these may be classed several other limestones of rather dull, earthy

* Strikes recorded from different parts are 10° S. of N.E., dip 85° north-westerly, and S.E., dip 75° south-westerly.

† T. G. Bonney, *Geol. Mag.*, 1890, decade 3, vol. vii. p. 536; and 1889, vol. vi. p. 483.

‡ Strike along south side of Throne glacier valley, 7½° S. of E.S.E., dip about vertical.

character: [248] and [249], from Gusherbrum (reddish), and [253], from near Golden Throne (mottled, red, and green), which is crushed and slaty.

The next group includes breccias, mostly of limestone. [242a], from close to summit of Crystal Peak (20,000 feet), consists mainly of crystals of quartz, but these adhere to a small piece of rock, which may perhaps be a brecciated limestone containing white and dark grey fragments. [226], from moraine on the Baltoro glacier, is a breccia of greyish, larger and dull green smaller fragments imbedded in a red-stained, calcareous matrix. A white mineral veins the rock; this, probably, is calcite, but with a hardness due to impurities. [256], from right of Throne glacier, includes sub-rounded fragments from blackish to pinkish or creamy-brown. [264], from moraine coming from west of Golden Throne, seems to be a limestone breccia somewhat modified by pressure. [301], from Golden Throne, is mainly calcareous, but on it is a greenish-greyish, sometimes silvery mineral incrustation, not improbably akin to agalmatolite. [225], from Baltoro glacier, is a dull red and green specimen with whitish veins, and [302], from Golden Throne, is a much crushed slaty rock of purple and green, the latter part rich in a carbonate. It is difficult to determine the precise origin of these two rocks; possibly they may be in reality crushed and decomposed felstones. [304], a dull purplish limestone much veined with white calcite, and [303], in which the vein calcite (some of it red-stained) dominates over the rock (grey), are both from the Golden Throne.

[185], by icefall, left bank of Shallihuru glacier (strike 5° S. of S.E., dip 75° south-westerly),* consists of fragments, one a crystalline marble, others finer-grained limestones, and one harder, probably a quartzite—all imbedded in a matrix partly calcareous. In this, mica probably fragmental is present, and a thin section shows a few minute rutiles. The rock has undergone crushing; this, however, has affected another specimen from the same place more strongly, [184], for it has produced a lamination. The powder of the last-named rock is unusually rich in small rutiles, one in a felspar crystal, and contains several prisms of a pale greenish, indigo-coloured mineral, more probably tourmaline than hornblende.

Some schistose calcareous grits come next. [258], from moraine coming from west foot of Golden Throne. Microscopic examination shows grains generally of quartz, occasionally composite, mostly irregular in outline, sometimes lenticular or slightly elongated, occurring at intervals along the laminæ of a very fine-grained ground-mass. This exhibits slightly undulate thin laminæ, partly of thin flakes of clear mica, partly of a more dusty material. They are separated by a granular aggregate, doubtless crushed, in which occasionally clearer calcite crystals occur close to a larger fragment, formed either by its *débris* or under its lee. Cubes of pyrite, and products which result from its oxidation, are present. The rock is a schistose calcareous grit. [268], from the same moraine, a purplish-grey schistose rock, seemingly an impure limestone modified by pressure, bears considerable resemblance to the last both in the hand specimen and under the microscope, but is not quite so distinctly crushed, though a kind of foliation is perceptible. It appears to include a fair-sized fragment of a quartz-felspar grit. Apparently related to the last two specimens, but much finer grained, is [271], from the same moraine. Examination under the microscope shows the general character of the matrix to be the same, though the grains of quartz, &c., run smaller in size. Apparently these rocks have derived part of their materials from a crystalline series, but are not themselves, strictly speaking, crystalline. A somewhat similar rock (micaceous and pale green), from the same moraine,

* Strike, Awkbassa (right side of glacier) is 5° N. of S.E., dip 80° south-westerly.

is [269]. The powder shows fibrous crystalline aggregates enclosing felspar, in which often kaolin is developed, a fair amount of a carbonate (like dolomite), both in the groundmass and in included fragments or "eyes," and a filmy, pale green mica (or chlorite?), probably secondary. The rock is apparently a crushed grit. [260], from the same moraine, is probably similar. It exhibits silvery micaceous surfaces, and includes some dolomite among the small crushed fragments. Crystals of chalcopyrite are deposited on one side. A slaty rock of rather crystalline aspect [148] from just beyond Gulmet stream, south bank of Hunza river (strike 10° to 20° S. of E., dip vertical),* is seen, when powdered, to contain brown mica, felspar, to which minute enclosed opacite sometimes gives a fibrous aspect, quartz (?), some calcite, rutile (?), and decomposition products. It is most probably a calcareous rock, containing crystalline detritus, and affected by pressure.

Argillite and Slate.

[234], from moraine below the junction of Piale and Baltoro glaciers, an almost black, flinty argillite, which, on examination with the microscope, discloses a number of rather oval fragments, mostly quartz, sometimes composite. They lie in a dark, fibrous-looking matrix obviously affected, like the fragments themselves, by pressure. The rock has a micro-foliation, some very minute biotite occurring among other constituents of secondary origin, but is not a true schist. Microscopically it resembles certain dark, slaty rocks—probably of Carboniferous age—in the Alps, but macroscopically is much more compact and flinty than they. Such a rock might be produced by the denudation of schists like [150]. [289], from Indus valley, below Himis, a somewhat flinty-looking, palish-green argillite, including some rather darker lenticular patches easily overlooked. The patches under the microscope appear to consist largely of some variety of viridite or chlorite, and the rock itself to be a mudstone, slightly tinted with the same mineral, and containing a few somewhat larger grains of quartz, &c. The specimen recalls to mind some of the older Palæozoic or latest Archæan rocks of Britain, and possibly consists partially of volcanic dust. [15], from water-rolled rock near Mykiel, a hard, rather flinty argillite, distinctly banded, without signs of cleavage. In the darker and dominant part numerous minute, rather angular chips probably felspar, are seen under the microscope scattered in a dull brown, finely granular, earthy-looking matrix. In the lighter bands these colourless chips are much more frequent, together also with some traces of epidote. Rather irregular clot-like spots of pyrite associated with dark stains are fairly frequent. A small vein traversing the slice is occupied mainly by a light-coloured mineral, which gives low polarisation tints, and is rather granular in structure, together with a glass-clear mineral, probably quartz, and occasional small quantities apparently of a carbonate. [251], from right bank of Throne glacier, is a black argillite with two directions of cleavage structure, as if from some crumpling.

[45], from Indus valley, near Bunji Bridge,† is a small subangular pebble of a compact dark rock, with hardness less than 6. The powder (greyish in colour) consists of felspar, often almost black with thickly disseminated opacite, (?) quartz, pale green hornblende, both fibrous and prismatic, with some pale green mica, (?) limonite, and tourmaline. The rock is probably a variety of argillite, slightly cleaved. [229], from Baltoro glacier,‡ is a

* About Gulmet the strike is practically parallel to valley, dip usually about 30° southerly.

† All the stones covering the floor of the valley have the slightly burnished iron-stained look of this specimen.—W. M. C.

‡ 229 forms with 227, 228 the bulk of moraine on left half of glacier.—W. M. C.

pale greyish-green rock, one part showing the effects of pressure much more markedly than the other. This may be due to the presence of bands of different texture in a sedimentary rock, or possibly to the junction of an igneous rock and a volcanic tuff, generally similar in composition. The powder contains fragments of a fibrous crystalline aggregate, some brown mica; in the less slaty, zircon (?) and a little iron oxide are present. [252], from Throne glacier,* a red, calcareous slate (imperfectly cleaved), possibly originally a fine ashy tuff, which apparently includes small grains of felspar, some at least being plagioclase.

[1], from Jhelam valley below Baramula, a purple-red argillaceous rock with a rather imperfect cleavage, which gives somewhat satiny surfaces. Under the microscope it shows small angular fragments of quartz interspersed with rather flattened grains, which appear to consist of very minute flakes or fibres of a micaceous mineral arranged roughly parallel to the longer axis. These are very likely felspar fragments altered in part by pressure; they are separated more or less by irregular lines of dull reddish granular dust. One or two fragmental grains resemble staurolite. Probably the rock was a fine-grained quartz-felspar grit which afterwards was affected by pressure and infiltrated by iron oxide. Macroscopically it bears some resemblance to inferior specimens of slate from the Glyn quarries, Llanberis. [290], from Indus valley below Himis, is a small piece of a fine gritty slate of a reddish-purple colour (like some of the Welsh slates) without the satiny look of the last specimen. [9], from *débris* at foot of slope at Mapnun, Burzil pass, is a bad purplish slate with a hälleflintoid band.

[212], from moraine from Ogre's Fingers. A compact, somewhat micaceous and finely-gritty, closely-cleaved rock of dark grey colour, exhibiting even laminæ with some much elongated lenticles. [3], from Jhelam valley below Baramula, is a similar compact, dark, rather gritty phyllite, the materials probably largely derived from crystalline rocks. The specimen breaks parallel with the planes of its micaceous constituent; there seem to be traces of a second cleavage making an oblique angle with the first. [250], from right bank of Throne glacier, a more micaceous lead-coloured phyllite, exhibiting V-shaped crumplings. [6], from Burzil valley at a bend near where the Kumri pass route leaves the Burzil pass route, is a similar phyllite, perhaps more micaceous, certainly more crushed, almost papery, crossed by minute "ruckings." [78], from moraine on left half of Gargo glacier between foot of glacier and Gargo. The powder shows felspar, much of a micaceous mineral, perhaps a little epidote, and opacite (sometimes as minute enclosures). The rock macroscopically is very fissile, with a minutely filmy silvery surface which is speckled with tiny dark spots—a phyllite rather than an ordinary slate. [122], a common rock in the left moraine of the Burchi glacier, is probably also a phyllite. The powder contains a filmy micaceous mineral, green aggregates with many specks of opacite and felspar. The rock is greyish with dark spots, and cleaved, not very different from the last one. [7], from the Burzil valley at the foot of the Kumri pass. A slaty rock of a rather black-lead colour and somewhat fibrous structure, the constituents being obviously minute. This, on microscopic examination, is seen to consist of microcrystalline white mica and quartz with streaky lines of opacite and some small needles of rutile. The rock obviously has been exposed to great pressure and exhibits strain-slip cleavage. Whether its present condition is to be ascribed to the dynamometamorphism of an ordinary argillaceous rock, or to the crushing of a dark schist such as those described from the Val

* 252 is associated both with 250, 251 from right bank, and with 257 from Golden Throne and from left bank of Throne glacier.—W. M. C.

Piora (Lepontine Alps),* cannot be easily determined; but it is more probably a phyllite.

SANDSTONES, GRITS AND CONGLOMERATE.

[164], common over the lower part of the right slope of Samaiyar valley. The powder contains clear felspar, colourless mica, some calcite, and probably rutile. The rock effervesces slightly with HCl, is a pale fawn colour, becoming browner in weathering, and appears to be a very fine-grained calcareous sandstone.

[272], from moraine from west foot of Golden Throne. A quartz grit of sub-rounded grains containing some felspar, rather rich in iron pyrites with a little copper pyrites. [277a], from medial moraine below Junction Camp, Baltoro glacier. A quartz-felspar grit on which is deposited some yellowish fluorspar. [204], characteristic of both moraines of Kero Lumba glacier, is a compact fine-grained quartz-sandstone, stained bright golden brown. The powder contains quartz, felspar, very rarely white and brown mica, some iron pyrite, and brownish translucent fragments with a minute, sub-parallel apparently tubular structure. [310], from left bank of Baltoro glacier, is a fine-grained whitish quartzose sandstone with some felspar and a quartz vein. [223], from the bed of the Baltoro river. A compact felspathic quartzose grit, of a dull reddish-purple colour, showing traces of a fine banding. The minerals are red-stained felspar, (?) quartz, and rarely a green mica. [230], from moraine on Baltoro glacier, is a purplish-red, fine-grained felsitic grit. The powder includes felspar, quartz, and red-stained fibrous crystalline aggregates, probably felspar or altered minerals. [179], a loose specimen from near Hunza, is a very small fragment of a fine-grained rock, whether a felsitic grit or a felstone it is almost impossible to determine. The matrix is dark from limonite staining, and the powder under the microscope contains some mica, (?) quartz, felspar, and (?) a zircon. [317], from near Askole, a small flattened pebble (with weathered-out veins forming ridges) of a rather dark-coloured, fine-grained grit, apparently cleaved. [247], from Gusherbrum, is a brownish-stained, dull, compact felspathic grit (rather like [317]). The minerals are chiefly felspar and quartz, much iron-stained. [228], forming with [227, 229] the bulk of the moraine on left half of Baltoro glacier, is a brown-stained, very compact grit, almost a quartzite.

Among the more markedly schistose gritty rocks are some rather ill-defined and veined purplish specimens from near the Golden Throne. [276], on the first point of the arête of Pioneer Peak as part of specimen [274], is mostly a vein of reddish calcite, with other ill-defined minerals. [265], from the moraine coming from western foot of the mountain, includes fragments of limestone in a purplish schistose matrix. [266], from same moraine, is a much squeezed purple, slaty rock, almost banded with narrow parallel calcareous veins.

Other cleaved specimens also from near Golden Throne are more micaceous. [275], from first point of arête forming junction with [274], occurs again at second peak (strike 5° E. of S., dip 35° easterly), has a purplish, well-cleaved matrix, perhaps somewhat resembling [223], but with silvery micaceous surfaces probably developed by pressure. It includes definite small pebbles, generally elliptical and flattened (the largest three-eighths of an inch long), some calcareous, one apparently a compact green quartzose grit. The powder contains felspar, some quartz, and a carbonate, and the rock is crossed by a vein of calcite. This specimen bears some resemblance to certain cleaved pebbly grits in the

* T. G. Bonney, Q. J. G. S., 1890, vol. xlvi. p. 199.

lower Cambrians of Wales. It is probably a grit not rich in quartz, of crystalline or igneous materials.

[267], from moraine coming from western foot of the mountain, is a well-cleaved schistose micaceous grit, in grain rather finer, in colour a silver grey. [158], from Samaiyar valley, characteristic of stones brought down from the west by avalanches. A very fine-grained pale grey or greenish-grey slaty mudstone, which, from its rather glimmering surface, seems to approach the phyllites. The powder is in angular fragments, mostly of clear minerals, a good deal of pale green mica, probably some pale greenish hornblende, felspar, and a black iron oxide, very probably ilmenite.

[270], from moraine coming from western foot of Golden Throne, is evidently crushed. A silvery lustre is given by minute (?) mica in a ground-mass, which varies in tint from bluish to violet-grey in changing lights. The powder contains grains often of quartz, fibrous aggregates including a micaceous mineral, specks of opacite and a prism of tourmaline. A thin slice shows the rock to be a quartz-felspar grit (some plagioclase), including several well-rounded grains, possibly also one or two bits from scoria. The interstitial dusty material consists largely of a very minute almost colourless mineral (? mica), which, as it happens, more commonly shows longish prismatic sections. These are about ·0008 inch in length. The rock is not unlike certain of the Cambrian grits of Britain.

The coarsest of these clastic rocks is—[10], from bank of stream by Mapnun, Bursil valley, a conglomerate consisting of rounded to angular (often greenish or reddish) fragments in a matrix which obviously contains volcanic materials. The largest fragment, quite an inch in diameter, is a speckled darkish-green colour. It is a holocrystalline rock consisting of quartz, felspar, a good deal of plagioclase (? oligoclase), with some orthoclase, occasionally idiomorphic, magnetite (with limonite), perhaps a little apatite, and a fair amount of green hornblende in irregular grains. The last is occasionally altered into a chlorite-like mineral, and may itself be a secondary product after augite. Thus the rock is a quartz-diorite, and its structure was affected in parts by mechanical disturbance before the pebble was made. Smaller fragments of many kinds of rock abound. These are chiefly volcanic, and vary apparently from basalts to andesites, dacites, or rhyolites. Several are amygdaloidal; the infilling material with the more basic is a rich green colour and has feeble action on polarised light. One fragment contains numerous lath-like felspar crystals, another of a speckled brown colour shows a slight fluidal structure, others seem to consist of a brown or greenish-brown glass partly altered. Fragments of coarser rocks contain plagioclase felspar, augite, and quartz; one or two are microgranite. A green (?) palagonitic mineral often forms a cement to the fragments. The materials of this conglomerate were probably obtained by the denudation of a volcanic region. It bears a rough resemblance to some of the Charnwood rocks and to those at or below the base of the Cambrian in North Wales.

Partially altered Sedimentary Rocks.

Two rocks show somewhat marked alteration. The first [161*c*], from a fallen fragment half-way between Samaiyar village and Strawberry Camp, on the left bank, is a blackish, compact, slightly-cleaved rock not distinctly crystalline, in which are scattered several crystalline grains, the largest slightly more than one-eighth of an inch in diameter. This has one fairly well-marked cleavage, with a sub-vitreous, slightly oily lustre, and a second more imperfect meeting it at an obtuse angle. The hardness seems to be slightly under 5. Under the microscope the ground-mass is seen to consist of minute films of a sericitic mica mixed with a minute colourless mineral and granules of opacite and ferrite. In this are scattered larger irregular grains and plates of a black mineral, with irregularly outlined flakes of biotite, containing much of the ground-mass, some prisms (probably rutile), and two or three specimens of a larger mineral (probably the same species as that already mentioned). The best-defined exhibits two cleavages, one better developed than the other, meeting at an angle of about 76°, and extinction takes place at an angle of 30° or a little less with the former. The crystals exhibit a rather irregularly-outlined prismatic form, the sides being roughly parallel with these cleavages. The crystals are crowded with minute materials apparently identical with the ground-mass. This presents a slight resemblance to that of the ottrelite rock of the Forges de la Commune, Ardennes, and of one or two schistose rocks from the Alps, which do not belong to the most ancient group. Both the biotite and the above-named mineral appear to have formed *in situ* at a time when molecular movements were not easy. We are unable to identify the latter with any mineral known to us, but it somewhat recalls to mind the "knoten and prismen" from certain pressure-rocks in the Lepontine Alps,* and even the couseranite from Vicdessos (Pyrenees). It does not seem to be tetragonal. We venture to suggest that it is a hydrous alumina-lime-silicate allied to the scapolite group. The matrix around the crystals is slightly coarser than elsewhere. Possibly the peculiarities in this rock may be the result of contact metamorphism.

[161*a*], from near Trough Camp, on right side of nevé (strike 7½° S. of E.S.E., dip 75° southerly). The rock obviously contains rather angular fragments of white marble imbedded in a hard matrix, grey speckled with dark green in colour. The larger marble fragments are stained externally with limonite, many of the smaller are altogether brown. Microscopic examination shows these to consist alike of crystalline calcite, fairly coarse in the whiter parts, fine-grained in the iron-stained. Both structures are sometimes present in the same fragment, and their relations suggest that the fine-grained one comes from a crushing of the coarser. The matrix has a sub-crystalline aspect, and is variable in character. In one part sub-angular grains of quartz appear to be, as it were, set in a matrix composed of small scales of mica (mostly white, but some green) and a chalcedonic material. This condition closely resembles that described in some Huronian conglomerates, and probably results from the alteration of a felspathic grit. In other parts a large grain of quartz is occasionally seen, commonly fairly well rounded, and the ground-mass consists of a mixture resembling that already described of minute mica with felspathic-looking granules, enclosing larger crystals of green and brown mica, and crystals of a prismatic mineral. These are fairly developed, rather elongated prisms, varying from about 1 : 4 to 1 : 8, up to·04 inch in length, rather full of microlithic enclosures, very pale yellowish-green with transmitted light, moderately bright-coloured with crossed nicols, and dichroism almost imperceptible. It shows a rather irregular transverse cleavage with occasional hints of one parallel to the edge, and extinguishes straight or nearly so with the sides of the prism. Though it has a general resemblance to epidote, the cleavage parallel with the bounding edges is not so marked as usual. It is, however, more like this mineral than andalusite, with specimens of which it has been compared. The mica, which occurs in flakes up to about ·11 inch in length, is dichroic, changing generally from a light straw colour to a brownish-green. It has formed after the epidote, and as it frequently borders the fragments of marble it may possibly be a lime-mica. As in slides [187, 188, 157], it gives the impression that it is slowly eating up the ground-mass. Of other minerals present in parts of the slice, rutile, sometimes in geniculate twins, is

* T. G. Bonney, Q. J. G. S., 1890, vol. xlvi. pp. 213-221.

rather abundant, and is included both in the epidote and in the mica. From its mode of occurrence a derivative origin seems probable. A few granules of iron oxide, apparently limonite, occur, also a rounded grain of zircon, and one small crystal of brownish tourmaline, secondary in origin.

Mineral or Vein Specimens.

The minerals include anhydrite, actinolite, a pseudo-jade, idocrase, noble serpentine, copiapite, and almandine; numerous examples of common garnets* (and others have been described among the rocks), many of epidote, tourmaline; also of pyrite, chalcopyrite, and other copper ores, usually in small amount. We have looked carefully for gold in the pyritiferous quartzose veins and other specimens, but have not detected any traces.

[232], from left half of Baltoro glacier, said to be rare. An angular fragment, partly limited by joints, of a variably greenish rock, irregularly mottled by a pale yellowish tint. The hardness is about 6·5, the s.g. 3·26, and the general appearance suggests a jade, but it differs in microscopic character from the few specimens of that rock which we have examined.† A slice exhibits in ordinary transmitted light a ground-mass of a very pale yellowish colour containing irregular dusty-looking patches and lines variable in their distribution. The parts freer from these enclosures are almost inert in polarised light, but contain at places a fibrous-flaky mineral extinguishing nearly straight, faintly polarising with dull olive-brown colours. This we find to correspond generally with the greener parts of the specimen. The more dusty parts (those corresponding macroscopically with the paler) exhibit in polarised light distinctly marked aggregates of very minute granules, and also a fibrous prismatic mineral, rather more brightly polarising, extinguishing at a fairly high angle, and having a somewhat matted arrangement, not improbably a pyroxene. There are some clustered granules and grains of a translucent brown mineral, seemingly isotropic, possibly a variety of garnet.

We have to thank Mr. P. Williams, of University College, for the following analysis made in Prof. Ramsay's laboratory :—

SiO_2	38·22
Al_2O_3	13·83
Fe_2O_3	7·81
CaO	25·55
MgO	3·73
K_2O	7·07
Na_2O	2·46
Loss at red-heat	1·89
	100·56

Microscopic examination, no less than chemical analysis, shows that this specimen cannot be referred to nephrite, and consists almost certainly of more than one mineral.

* A collection filling a small bag [325] was brought from near Tashot.

† General McMahon has been good enough to examine the slide and to give us the benefit of his experience of Indian rocks, determining at the same time the specific gravity, and making a qualitative analysis.

But it is very difficult to ascertain what these may be. The microscope does not give much help, for it indicates an aggregate of ill-defined constituents, which sometimes recall the structures seen in examining the material named saussurite. The chemical analysis is remarkable for its richness in lime and alkalies (especially potash) and comparatively low percentages of silica and alumina. The general character of the rock suggests the possibility of jadeite being an important, if not the main constituent. But according to Krenner * the normal analysis of this mineral is $SiO_2=50\cdot23$, $Al_2O_3=25\cdot37$, $Na_2O=15\cdot40$; and though the actual analyses of specimens (doubtless being rather mixtures) have generally somewhat more silica and less alumina and soda, with a little lime and protoxide of iron, still they do not correspond with the present one. Apart from the difficulty of the presence of so much potash, we should find, if we supposed the alkalies to be present in jadeite, hardly any silica or alumina left for the lime and other protoxide constituents. Saussurite would account for some of the alkalies and of the lime, but has nearly the same silica percentage as jadeite and a rather higher one of alumina. Zoisite (proper), epidote, the scapolite group, and elæolite, present, in each case, important differences. Certain of the constituents agree fairly well with a lime-garnet.† The rock in which this occurs is said to be homogeneous, tough, with a rather waxy lustre, and a yellowish-white colour; hardness $=7$, and s.g. $=3\cdot33$–$3\cdot64$. It gave on analysis, $SiO_2=44\cdot85$, $Al_2O_3=10\cdot76$, $Fe_2O_3=3\cdot20$, $CaO=34\cdot38$, $MgO=5\cdot24$; loss by ignition, 1·10; total, 99·53. And of this Dr. Hunt takes for the garnet, $SiO_2=22\cdot69$, $Al_2O_3=10\cdot76$, $Fe_2O_3=3\cdot20$, $CaO=21\cdot07$; total, 57·72. Such a mineral as this, if present in considerable quantity, would leave in the Karakoram rock a fair amount of silica for the alkalies and remaining protoxide bases. A mineral resembling a pyroxene seems to be present. On the whole, after consulting many analyses of rocks and minerals, we venture to suggest that this rock may be composed of a lime-garnet, a potash jadeite, a mineral of the scapolite group, and a little pyroxene (or possibly even wollastonite or pectolite). It is more probably a vein product, for the low percentage of alumina seems to exclude a euphotide consisting mainly of felspar.

[190], from the right moraine of the Samaiyar Bar glacier, consists of white intercrystallised calcite and anhydrite; [324], from fallen quartz block, Gander Chish, Hispar glacier, are pale green prisms ($\frac{3}{16}$ inch across) of a form of actinolite, not quite pure, containing some calcite. The powdered fragments under the microscope have the character of actinolite, but in one or two the extinction is high, so that some omphacite may be included in the specimens. Two specimens come from Biafo glacier (right moraine).‡ One [215] of grass-green actinolite in rather small crystals, intercrystallised with a brownish mica in variable quantities, shows signs of mechanical disturbance; it may be a rock specimen. The other [216] consists of rather large crystals of grass-green actinolite, passing into a practically colourless, more asbestiform variety, with one or two films of a golden mica, and a grey mineral, also pyroxenic. From on or near the Baltoro glacier come [281], from medial moraine, Bruce's Camp, idocrase in part intercrystallised with a pale green mineral, a (?) variety of sahlite; [277b], from right bank above Corner Camp, vein specimen of quartz, felspar (like oligoclase), and white mica, with red garnet (almandine) intercrystallised with the quartz, forming a very rude network. Also two specimens of noble serpentine; they are sub-translucent, of yellowish-green colour, with

* "Neues Jahrb. fur Min.," 1883, ii. p. 173.

† T. S. Hunt, "Amer. Journ. Sci.," xxvii. (1859), p. 342.

‡ See note on 213, 214.

red patches in [236], from a medial moraine, and with adherent calcareous fragment in [245], from "thin seams in a green mass" on the ascent to White Fan pass.

(Epidote.) Well crystallised prisms of epidote occur in a vein of quartz in [17], from a fallen block at Mykiel. The powder of the adherent rock contains felspar, not much quartz, a (?) hexagonal chlorite, and epidote, apparently connected with the chlorite, in small patches. The rock appears as if it might be akin to a rather quartzose diorite, and as if the chlorite (with epidote) replaced a hornblende. In [66], from Bagrot glacier, the epidote crystals form radiating or spherulitic clusters (½ inch) in a vein in what appears to be a diorite containing minute epidote. [72], from Gargo glacier, consists mainly of intercrystallised diverging prisms of epidote and (?) calcite, with felspar, a little mica, and specks of (?) opacite. Four specimens coloured by minute epidote may be only vein products. The powder both of [95], from the right moraine, and of [100], from the left, of Gargo glacier contains a large amount of epidote and also of fine fibrous hornblende or actinolite. In [89], from the left moraine, the dominant minerals are epidote and a chlorite apparently hexagonal, with felspar and possibly quartz. [138], from a 4-inch seam in right bank of valley near Sinakar, consists very largely of finely granular epidote, some felspar, with an admixture at one part of a little hornblende, producing a darker streak or band.

(Tourmaline.) This mineral occurs in many specimens. Crystals (½ inch across) collected out of the vein [197], from right of Hispar valley between the bridges, resemble those obtained from Monte Rosa, but the Karakoram prisms are somewhat irregularly broken across. From Gargo glacier (left) come [91], minute schorl (with some brownish quartz), the dichroism being from almost colourless to bluish-grey or black; and [92], yellow-stained quartz with clear crystals partly coated with minute limonite; schorl occurs in nests, and some pierces the quartz. In [174], from Rash ridge, part of the white vein-quartz is coloured by schorl. [115], from Burchi glacier, consists of quartz, acicular schorl, a little chalcopyrite, minute silvery mica, and perhaps a little dolomite. [84], from Gargo glacier, is a small specimen of quartz with aggregated chlorite, a very little schorl, and some cupriferous pyrite. [189], from between Shallihuru and Samaiyar Bar glaciers, contains quartz, some tourmaline, pyrite, chalybite, and (?) dolomite, with minute reticulate rutile (sagenite) as figured by Rosenbusch,* the individual prisms being ⅛ inch or more in length. A fragment adhering is a much-crushed mica schist, of pale silvery mica with a little of a sienna-brown variety of biotite, and containing schorl needles.

(Quartz, &c.) Rock crystal occurs in [319], and with enclosed mineral in [320], both from near Askole. [99] from Gargo glacier (left), and [106] from Emerald Peak; also [40] and [41] (red-stained) and [39], all three from below Hatu Pir; and [311] from Baltoro glacier, dark, with limonite, all consist of crystalline quartz. [63], from Bagrot glacier (left side), is a flake, probably crushed vein, green-stained. Some mica occurs with the quartz; it is only a little in [196], of a pale greenish silvery colour in [197], both from Hispar valley between the bridges, clearly intercrystallised in [312], from Baltoro glacier, and with small clear brown prisms of quartz and specks of black iron oxide in [92], from Gargo glacier sub-rounded). The mica forms pseudo-hexagonal flakes with clear prisms of quartz in [205], from Hispar glacier, and is associated also with white felspar in [24], from Astor valley. [211], from Biafo glacier, a whitish quartz felspar vein, contains dull green aggregates consisting of minute mica (? hexagonal). Prisms of clear quartz are found with small scalenohedra of calcite in [305], from Golden Throne, and with minute flattened rhombo-

* "Micr. Petrogr. of Rock-forming Minerals" (J. P. Iddings), p. 146, fig. 58.

hedra (nail-head spar), in a confused heavy mass [239], from Baltoro glacier, containing some (?) chalybite and iron oxide, and fairly rich in a very minute black mineral, probably galena.

Chalybite often occurs with quartz, forming in [132], from Dar, a small vein with a little limonite. [88], from Gargo glacier, contains also mica and indications of other iron compounds. [177], from Samaiyar Bar glacier, consists of quartz (with some carbonate, minute mica, and a little chlorite), includes chalybite and pyrite (some small, and a partly decomposed larger crystal). [74], from Gargo glacier, consists of quartz, mica, chalybite, chlorite, and felspar slightly green-stained. [263], two specimens, are vein quartz with some limonite, chalcopyrite, and white mica (with chalybite in one, calcite in the other), apparently from a crushed chlorite schist; [262], with chalybite, and [261] contain pyrite, limonite, and a black substance, possibly from decomposition of the pyrite. All these specimens are from Golden Throne moraine. [129], from yellow stratum at foot of Dar valley, has a powdery white crust at places, formed over a yellow mineral, which proves to consist chiefly of ferric sulphate. It appears to be copiapite, and may have been formed by decomposition of iron pyrite which occurs in adjacent rocks from this locality. The paper enclosing the specimen has been partially corroded.

The next specimens consist of vein quartz with pyrite and sometimes limonite; four from left of Throne glacier [313], with some marcasite apparently in a chloritic schist; two [156] from Samaiyar valley containing a black mineral, in one probably wad, in the other minute blende; [98], from Gargo glacier with greenish (?) chlorite, silvery mica, a little of a carbonate, and some chalcopyrite; [273], much crushed, and [306], with a filmy (?) micaceous layer, both from Golden Throne. [69] consists of a quartz vein in a crystalline rock containing epidote, a large grain of pyrite, and probably magnetite; [75] is a crystal of chalcopyrite: both these are from Gargo glacier. [286], from moraine east of Skoro La, consists of pyrite cubes on the surface of a slabby piece of whitish rock, probably a gneiss. The powder contains felspar, mica, rutile, and probably some apatite. In [321], from near Askole, the streak indicates hematite, but the specimen is light in weight, as if some other mineral may have been removed.

Traces of various ores of copper are fairly numerous. From Burchi glacier comes vein quartz, more or less stained with malachite, in [109] containing also chalcopyrite, perhaps melaconite, possibly a little chalybite; in [110] with brown dendritic markings, possibly an ore of copper; in [112] and [114] with schorl and what appears to be chalcopyrite and melaconite; in [113] also with schorl; and in [111] including a crushed micaceous layer. From Gargo glacier (left side) come [96], of quartz, with silvery mica and traces of copper ore, and [70]. This, like [135], from Bagrot glacier, has a greenish layer, (?) chloritic, some chalcopyrite and specks of malachite; and in the latter are also melaconite, and probably cuprite. [146], from opposite Chalt, is a crushed vein, green-stained. [26], from west side of Astor valley, near Astor, is a small fragment of dioritic rock (plagioclase felspar, hornblende) stained with copper ore, which looks more like chrysocolla. In two specimens the copper ore is associated with dolomite; it consists in [322], from near Askole, of melaconite, partly coated with malachite, and in [235], from medial moraine of Baltoro glacier, of malachite, probably with a copper oxide, with a little (?) galena; and in [144], from near Chalt, it stains a crushed (?) chloritic rock traversed by a vein, probably dolomite.

Calcite occurs in [323], from near Askole, as short prisms terminated by blunt rhombohedra (with pale green mica), forming a crumbling mass, which covers a fairly thick flake; and as rhombohedra, with minute chlorite, in [76], from Gargo glacier, and with quartz and aggregated biotite (a variety) in [181], from near Mir. [274], from the arête on the ascent to Pioneer Peak (adjoining the pebbly grit 275), is an irregular crushed lump of impure calcite, including small greenish (?) chloritic patches, possibly fragments. This may perhaps be a rock specimen rather than a vein. [255], from right of Throne glacier, is a very compact dolomite stained with ferric oxide and possibly a trace of manganese.

Specimens, which are mainly limonite, in some cases may be decomposed and stained rock fragments, but consist of vein quartz in [125], in [131] (with mica), both from foot of Dar valley, and in [123] (with mica), from Burchi glacier. [60], from Bagrot glacier, may be vein or quartzose grit. [55] (brown and red) and [57], from Bagrot valley, and [307], from Golden Throne, appear to be fine-grained crystalline rocks much stained. [134] is probably also a rock fragment. It shows silvery micaceous surfaces, both parallel and roughly perpendicular to a close lamination, and may be a crushed gneiss or schist. From Gargo glacier [85] (and similarly [81]) is a decomposed rock specimen. It contains abundant small pyrite and chalcopyrite, and effervesces slightly with HCl, but so far as can be seen it more resembles a fine-grained gneiss. [124], from foot of Dar valley, is a decomposed earthy rock, enclosing fragments varying in size and shape, some being dull green, which prove to be chiefly an aggregate of mica, either green or becoming brown by alteration. The rock adhering to a red-stained quartz vein in [33] and in [34], from *débris* north of Doian, Astor valley, is clearly a fragment of micaceous gneiss.

Geographical Distribution.

[*Specimens marked * were obtained in situ.*]

We pass next to the geographical distribution of the rocks mentioned in the preceding list. Mr. Conway's collection commences with some specimens from the Jhelam valley below Baramula. These are a limestone and slates, not unlike some which occur in the Secondary series of the Alps. The next specimens are from Gurai, in the side valley north of the Tragbal pass. These (fallen blocks) are granite and diorite. Advancing thence up the valley of the Kishanganga and the Burzil valley, *phyllites, a *conglomerate and then a *granite were collected, and fallen blocks near Mapnun furnished a slate and a serpentine. Descending from the Burzil pass towards the Astor valley, *hornblende diorite and *chlorite schist were found; in fallen blocks diorites and a micaceous gneiss; and one water-rolled specimen of argillite. Near Astor, two varieties of gneiss were obtained from boulders. Below Astor, a *diorite on the west of the river, and apparently also on the east, and fallen blocks of hornblendite on the west, a *garnetiferous gneiss (near Parri), common as big boulders down the valley; and then *granulite and *fine-grained gneiss (these two abundant by the roadside). The strikes and dips recorded by Mr. Conway in some cases may be rather planes of jointing, and in other crystalline masses are most probably to be reckoned as results of pressure. Down to this part of the Astor valley the strikes vary from 15° W. of N. to 10° E. of N., the dips varying from 30° eastward to vertical. From the lower part of the valley, and from below Hatu Pir, come *micaceous gneisses, and *diorite at Ramghat. In the valley the strikes vary from N.N.E. to nearly N.E., the dips being on the south-eastern side from 30° to 45°, while below Hatu Pir the strike varies between 10° N. or S. of E., the dips being 33° on the southern side.

The first specimens brought by Mr. Conway from the valley of the Indus come from the neighbourhood of Bunji. They are *granite, hornblendite, decomposed diabase, and micaceous gneiss. The next specimens are representatives of the Bagrot valley, which enters the Gilgit (a tributary of the Indus), carrying the drainage of a line of lofty peaks and their southern spurs, which curve round from Rakipushi on the west to Emerald Peak on the east. From below Sinakar, in the lower part of the Bagrot valley, comes a *hornblende schist, the general strike being nearly E.N.E., dip northerly 55°, and a *diorite. Hence to a fork in the valley near the foot of the Bagrot glacier, the specimens represent apparently *crushed gneiss, and diorites of more than one kind. *One of these is said to extend far along the valley; others are common in the *débris*. Some strikes are recorded to easterly or east-north-easterly points, but the dips vary. The Bagrot glacier issues from a loop of peaks, and Mr. Conway remarks that the mountains on the western side of the glacier as far as Rakipushi consist of hornblende rocks, like those of the Bagrot valley. From the ridge he collected a *crushed gneiss, and from the Kamar nala beyond a crushed *quartzose mica schist. On the eastern side of the glacier were collected a calcareous *sillimanite schist and a *hornblende schist, the latter being pretty certainly a crushed doleritic rock and not unlike some of the "grüner schiefer" of the Alps. From the glacier come a diorite, common in the left moraine, and a crushed mica schist. Passing up the eastern fork, Mr. Conway collected a *hornblende schist or pressure-modified diorite, a *mica diorite, some *sericite schists, before reaching the foot of the Burchi glacier, which, descending from the north, joins the yet larger Gargo glacier. The specimens from near the former represent a crushed *calc-mica schist (*in situ* on the spur between the two glaciers) and (from the left moraine) an impure limestone, a phyllite, and a diorite—so that there must be here an infold of comparatively unaltered rock. From the other glacier a crushed *actinolitic schist occurs on the left bank of the valley beyond Gargo; yet further up on this side comes a *gneiss (crushed). The glacier was now crossed again to the slopes beneath Emerald Peak, on the ascent of which *sericite and *chlorite schist were obtained. The right moraine of the Gargo glacier furnishes sericite schists, the left moraine or left side piedmontite schists, chlorite schist, diorite, hornblende schist or schistose diorite, calc-mica schist, phyllite, and from an old moraine another diorite. Piedmontite schist also comes from a boulder further down the valley on the left side. The exact locality where this interesting rock occurs *in situ* is not determined, but it is clearly somewhere in the buttresses of the Gargo peaks. These are part of a huge spur which extends from the Emerald Peak to Dubanni. The strikes along the Gargo valley from the fork are generally between 5° S. of E. to 7° S. of E.S.E., the dips on the south side of the valley and on a peak east of Gargo northward from 40° to 80° or vertical, on the north side of the valley southward 60°. On the hill above the icefall, however (left side), and on Emerald Peak, the strike is N. of E.N.E., the dip southerly 30° to 75°.

The next set are from the valley leading to the Gilgit river from Chalt. The geology of this region was investigated by Surgeon Captain Giles. Here Mr. Conway took only a few specimens (*diorites and *hornblendite), and remarks that the rocks are similar to those of the Bagrot valley. Approaching and passing Chalt, *crystalline limestone *in situ*, and a *chloritic rock occur; the strike of these varies from 8° N. of S.E. to 13° S. of E., the dips being northerly from 50° to 85°. It is noted that much nearer Gilgit the strike of the rocks was E., the dip varying, and that on going northward it bends round to be a little more nearly in the direction of the valley.

The next set of specimens represent the rocks between Gulmet and Shaiyar; they are *schistose calcareous grit, *fine-grained gneiss (both sides of river), a *granulite, a *crystalline limestone, a *micaceous gneiss (at Shaiyar), and as loose specimens, garnets, common near the crystalline limestone, a felstone (Gulmet), and black garnet-schist (abundant), the last bearing some resemblance to a rock in the Lepontine Alps, on the southern side. It is highly probable that we have in this region, as in parts of the Lepontine Alps, a series of gneissic rocks overlain by a group of crystalline schists, probably metamorphosed sediments, over which comes a late series of comparatively unaltered strata. The strikes at this part are stated to be "parallel with the valley near Gulmet, dipping at 30° in a southerly direction;" above this they vary apparently from E.N.E. to E.S.E., the dips being generally on the southern side, from 20° to vertical.

In the Samaiyar valley, below the glacier, are *a fine-grained gneiss, *granite (left side, west of camp), and, from fallen fragments on the same side, a schistose dipyr rock, crystalline limestone, a mica schist (with some secondary mica), and a schistose grit (brought down abundantly by avalanches). The character of these rocks suggests the possibility that the granite is intrusive in the sedimentaries. The strikes in this part of the valley vary from 5° N. of N.E. to 7° S. of S.E., the dips being very high, generally from 85° to vertical. Along the Samaiyar glacier, on the left bank, is a *somewhat micaceous gneiss. On the right, near Trough Camp, a *micaceous conglomerate, which recalls some rocks of Huronian age in Canada. On the same side, near the east end of "Trough Saddle," a *fine-grained gneiss (common down the left moraine of the glacier). The strikes below Trough Camp are between E.S.E. and 10° S. of S.E., dip southerly 55° to 80°, but at the east end of "Trough Saddle" the strike is nearly N.N.E., the dip vertical.

After returning to the Nagyr valley and ascending to Hopar, there come, beyond it, a *fine-grained gneiss, a *mica-diorite and as loose specimens along the left side of the Nagyr valley and of the Bualtar glacier (apparently from the Crown of Dirran) diorites; from the medial moraine of the glacier a granite, and from the right one a "number of rocks similar to those of the Bagrot valley." The strike below Nagyr is 10° N. of S.E., dip northerly 75°, but south of Hopar the strikes vary from 5° S. of S.E., dip southerly 30° (several places) to 7° S. of E.S.E., dip southerly 50°. Along the Shallihuru glacier, at and above Mir Camp, come a *fine-grained gneiss, a *crushed mica schist, a *calcareous mica schist, a *limestone breccia (left bank), and from the Dasskaram Needle a *fine-grained gneiss, and a *mica schist with secondary mica [187, 188]. A fine-grained gneiss is recorded as common in the Mir moraine, and said by Mr. Conway to correspond with that in the "Trough Saddle." The strikes along the valley and on Dasskaram Needle vary from 5° S. of S.E. to 15° N. of S.E., the dips being south-westerly from 75° to 85°. From the Samaiyar Bar glacier come a crushed mica schist (left side), and a crushed calc schist (right moraine). The Rash ridge on the right bank of the Barpu glacier was climbed in more than one place. The eastern face consists of a *garnetiferous gneiss, *crystalline limestone, and a *mica diorite forming all the upper part of the ridge; the more western part of *garnetiferous gneiss and (?) *kinzigite, *micaceous gneiss, *banded gneiss, and a *diorite ("forming a thin vein at the top of the ridge"). The ridge thus must consist very largely of gneissic rocks, which, however, probably are pressure-modified igneous rocks. The strike is recorded as from 10° to 25° S. of S.E., the dips varying, above Barpu Camp being southerly 30° to 60°.

In ascending by the long Hispar glacier to the pass of the same name the following rocks were collected: a *fine-grained gneiss on Shukurri near the foot of the glacier, also abundant in the moraine, and a *micaceous gneiss (left bank); and on the right (nearly three-fifths of the way up) a *granite, which according to Mr. Conway is common down the right moraine, and considerably higher up (camp by Hispar Snowfield) a *micaceous gneiss. The strikes vary from 2° N. of E.S.E. to 10° S. of E.S.E.; the dips recorded from the lower part of the glacier, on the left bank, are vertical and 75° southerly, from the upper end, right bank, vertical and 60° northerly. The loose specimens are (in fallen blocks), from the right bank below Shukurri a micaceous gneiss, from the left on Haigutum slopes a banded gneiss (common); also a sandstone characteristic of the moraine of the Kero Lumba glacier, and from the right moraine a fine-grained gneiss (common). Evidently the rocks on either side of this huge ice sheet are crystalline, but an infolded mass of comparatively unaltered sedimentaries must exist somewhere among the peaks to the south.

In the descent over the Biafo glacier from this pass a *gneissoid granite was found on the right side at Snow Lake Camp (the first halting-place), the structure striking 10° N. of E., dipping 60° northerly, then at "Ogre's Camp" (on the same side), and again at Nambla Camp, near the lower end of the glacier, a *micaceous gneiss, in the former place striking 5° N. of S.E., dipping 80° on the southern side. From the left bank, at the foot of Latok glacier (eastern angle), comes a *granite, which according to Mr. Conway forms the bulk of the *débris*. Moraine specimens are: granite (the rock which "appears to form the needles"), fine-grained gneiss, crushed micaceous gneiss, and two specimens of crystallised actinolite (these, however, may be only vein products) (right side), and a slate (obtained a few yards from Ogre's Camp).

From the valley of the Biaho, rather west of the entrance of that from the Biafo glacier, comes (near Askole) a *mica diorite, and as loose fragments, a garnetiferous (?) quartzite, two varieties of garnet schist, one which is water-worn, of the black kind already mentioned, the other containing chlorite and green mica, also a crystalline dolomite and a fine-grained sandstone. On the ascent to Skoro La (roughly south of Askole) a *micaceous gneiss was collected. The specimens indicate that the rocks enclosing the Biafo glacier correspond generally with those on the west side of the Hispar pass, and that the belt of sedimentaries, already noted as occurring somewhere among the mountains on the left bank of the Hispar glacier, possibly is prolonged into those on the right bank of the Biafo glacier.

A rather large valley descends into the Biaho valley, carrying the drainage of the Punmah glacier, and separated from the one occupied by the Biafo glacier by a spur-like range of lofty mountains. The western side of the extremity of this contains *crystalline dolomite and a *fine-grained gneiss, the eastern side a *crystalline limestone, a *hornblende schist, a *fine-grained gneiss, and a *garnetiferous mica schist. The strike of the dolomite on the one side and of the limestone on the other is 11° S. of S.E., the dip being 40° towards the south-west. Ascending the Biaho valley above the junction with that bringing the water from the Punmah glacier, Mr. Conway obtained, just at the angle between them, a *fine-grained gneiss, striking 5° N. of S.E., and dipping 70° on the south-westerly side. Near the foot of the Baltoro glacier, above the camp, comes a *granite and a sandstone from blocks in the bed of the river. By this glacier on the north side were *granite, a *fine-grained gneiss (into which apparently the granite is intrusive), a *crystalline limestone, the second striking 7° S. of S.S.E., dipping 10° on the western side, the third striking 10° N. of E., dipping 85° southerly, but with many contortions. On the south side *granites, of which, according to Mr. Conway, the mountains rising on this side of the lower part of the glacier consist. The moraine on the right bank furnished an ordinary limestone, a black argillite, and a crystalline limestone; the medial one a fine-grained gneiss, a sandstone, a slaty (? felsitic) tuff, a limestone, a pseudo-jade (marked as rare), three specimens (of which the bulk of the moraine is said to consist), viz., a crushed gneiss, a sandstone, and a slate.

About this point a marked change takes place in the scenery. From the higher part of the Biafo glacier the mountains are characterised by needle forms; further to the east, though lofty, they are more rounded in outline. In this part Crystal Peak rises on the right bank of the Baltoro glacier. From its southern slopes come (order uncertain) *fine-grained gneiss, a *calcitic quartz schist, a *dark mica schist, *dolomite, and *limestone, both crystalline), a *fine-grained gneiss, and another one crumpled. A specimen from the summit of Crystal Peak unfortunately consists mainly of crystallised quartz, but this adheres to a brecciated rock, some fragments in which effervesce a little, and may be limestone. The mass of practically unaltered sedimentary rock, of which the moraine has already given ample evidence, may therefore include the Crystal Peak. On the ascent to White Fan pass, south-east of the same peak, were collected a *mica syenite, a crystalline but fine-grained *white dolomite. A greyish *crystalline limestone occurs, it is said, apparently belonging to a mass of green rock, in which are thin seams of *noble serpentine. Half way up to this pass the strike is recorded as S.E., the dip being 75° to the south-west. A *diorite comes from the angle peak, *i.e.*, that which rises from the above-named mass west of the Godwin-Austen glacier.

The moraines from Gusherbrum give a sandstone and earthy limestones. The right bank of the Throne glacier *phyllite, *argillite, *limestone (these three being associated), *slate, and a *limestone breccia (this, however, might be a fault product). From the left bank of the same glacier (whether *in situ* is uncertain) a fine-grained gneiss, a granite, and a dolomite (the last is said also to occur in Golden Throne). The strike in the mountains by the glacier is said to be 70° S. of E.S.E. (dip about vertical), and this continues all along the valley. The moraine starting from the western foot of Golden Throne affords sandstone, grits, and calcareous grits (both schistose), limestones and dolomite, and the peculiar felstones described above. Mr. Conway states that the last named occur on the mountain and appear to form bands in the schistose grits. On the Pioneer Peak the first point of the arête reached yielded schistose grits, one of which (a purple specimen, with small pebbles) occurred again at the second peak, striking 5° E. of S., and dipping 35° to the east. It is evident that a considerable mass of sedimentary rock must be infolded from Gusherbrum to Golden Throne.

The valley of the Indus from Parkatta to Tolti (roughly S.S.W. of the district last described) lies among alternating *diorite and "granites." Higher up, from Himis to the turn for Lama-yuru, among *argillite and *slate (just like the redder slate of Llanberis), said by Mr. Conway to be "sandwiched" with granite.

Again and again throughout this district of the Karakorams, rocks bear evidence of severe pressure, the result of earth movements. Putting aside those which are either certainly or probably of igneous origin, we find three rather well-marked groups. One, fine-grained, speckled, gneisses, very similar to those which occur on the south side of the Central Highlands of Scotland (*e.g.*, about Blair Athol); secondly, crystalline schists, limestones and dolomites, doubtless metamorphosed sedimentaries, several of which are practically identical with specimens described by one of us from the Lepontine and Pennine Alps; † and, thirdly, a group of sedimentary rocks (not more than mechanically altered), sometimes also very like the Mesozoic rocks of the Alps, though occasionally some have a rather more ancient aspect. With these the peculiar felstones of the Golden Throne appear to be associated, and in one or two places the presence of somewhat altered fragmental rocks is suggested. It seems probable that the history of the Karakoram region is very similar to that of the Alps. First a great floor of crystalline rock, partly igneous, partly metamorphic, in the more strict sense of the word, on which was laid down, possibly with interruptions, and marked intervening disturbances and denudations, a series of sedimentary rocks. This ended, all were affected by a process of folding on a gigantic scale and upreared into a mountain mass, which has been carved by the usual agents of denudation into peaks and valleys far surpassing in wildness and grandeur even those of the Alps.

† T. G. Bonney, Q. J. G. S., 1890, vol. xlvi. p. 187; and 1893, vol. xlix. p. 89.

PLANTS.

PLANTS.

At the suggestion of the Director of the Royal Gardens, Kew, I made, with the help of Mr. McCormick, a carefully localised collection of dried plants. These we presented to Kew. I am indebted to the Director, Mr. Thiselton-Dyer, F.R.S., for the following list of determinations, which was made by a member of the Kew staff, Mr. W. Botting Hemsley, F.R.S.

Name.	Place.	Height in Feet.
Ranunculaceæ.		
Anemone albana, Stev.	Sat	c. 9,000
Callianthemum cachemirianum, Camb.	Sat	c. 9,000
Ranunculus hyperboreus, Rottb. var. *natans*, Regel	Barpu	c. 10,000
	Mir Pool	11,630
Ranunculus rubrocalyx, Regel ...	Gandar	13,070
	Haigutum	13,880
Isopyrum grandiflorum, Fisch. (much reduced)	Above Trough Camp	c. 16,000
Delphinium Brunonianum, Royle ...	Pool Camp	14,780
Aconitum Napellus, L. var. *rotundifolium*, Hk. f. and T....	Mango Brangsa	12,600
Berberidaceæ.		
Berberis vulgaris, L.	South slope, Rash ridge	c. 13,000
Papaveraceæ.		
Papaver nudicaule, L.	Left bank, Hispar glacier	c. 12,000
Fumariaceæ.		
Corydalis Govaniana, Wall	Left bank, Hispar glacier	c. 12,000
Corydalis crassifolia, Royle	Right bank, Baltoro glacier	c. 14,500
Corydalis tibetica, Hk. f. and T.... ...	(?)	
Cruciferæ.		
Parrya exscapa, Ledeb.	Dasskaram Needle	c. 16,500
Draba stenocarpa, H. f. and T. ...	Gilgit Road, Astor to Doian	c. 8,000
	Sat	c. 9,000
Draba tibetica, H. f. and T. (very much reduced)	Pool Camp	14,780

Name.	Place.	Height in Feet.
Cruciferæ (*continued*).		
***Draba incompta*, Stev. (?)**	**South slope, Rash ridge**	**c. 13,000**
***Draba glacialis*, Adams**	**South slope, Rash ridge**	**c. 13,000**
Draba* near *D. alpina	**Left bank, Hispar glacier**	**c. 12,000**
***Draba incana*, L.**	**Near Strawberry Camp**	**c. 11,000**
***Malcolmia africana*, R. Br. (two varieties)**	**Nagyr**	**7,790**
	Hunnuno, Hopar	**c. 12,000**
	Rash ridge	**13,400**
***Cochlearia Conwayi*, Hemsl. sp. n.**	**Hatu Pir**	**c. 10,000**
***Sisymbrium mollissimum*, C. A. M. var.**	**Moraine near Gargo**	**c. 11,500**
***Conringia planisiliqua*, F. and M.**	**Nagyr to Hopar**	**c. 8,500**
***Braya rosea*, Bunge**	**South slope, Rash ridge**	**c. 13,000**
***Brassica campestris*, L.**	**Askole**	**10,360**
***Capsella Bursa pastoris*, Medic.**	**Nagyr**	**7,790**
	Hopar	**9,220**
***Chorispora sabulosa*, DC.**	**Left bank, Hispar glacier**	**13,500**
***Chorispora sibirica*, Ledeb.**	**Gilgit Road, Astor to Doian**	**c. 8,000**
	Dirran	**9,500**
	Sat	**c. 9,000**
***Cheiranthus himalaicus*, Camb.**	**Moraine above Windy Camp**	**c. 12,700**
	Above Trough Camp	**c. 16,000**
	Dasskaram Needle	**c. 16,500**
***Thlaspi alpestre*, L.**	**Moraine above Strawberry Camp**	**c. 12,000**
	Nagyr	**7,790**
	Rash ridge	**13,400**
Capparidaceæ.		
***Capparis spinosa*, L.**	Hatu Pir	c. 10,000
Violaceæ.		
***Viola Patrinii*, DC.**	**Gilgit Road, Astor to Doian**	**c. 8,000**
***Viola canina*, L.**	**Moraine above Strawberry Camp**	**c. 12,000**
Caryophyllaceæ.		
Saponaria Vaccaria*, L. β. *grandiflora	**Askole**	**10,360**
***Silene Moorcroftiana*, Wall.**	**Nambla Brangsa**	**11,700**
***Silene conoidea*, L.**	**Hopar**	**9,220**
	Askole	**10,360**
***Lychnis brachypetala*, Edgew. and Hk. f.**	**South slope, Rash ridge**	**c. 13,000**
	Left bank, Hispar glacier	**c. 13,500**
***Cerastium trigynum*, Vill.**	**Mir**	**11,630**
	Boggy Camp	**13,570**
***Lychnis apetala*, L.**	**Pool Camp**	**14,780**
	Footstool Camp	**16,430**
***Stellaria Webbiana*, Wall.**	**Mir**	**11,680**
	Boggy Camp	**13,570**
***Arenaria holosteoides*, Edgew.**	**Nagyr to Hopar**	**c. 8,500**
Tamaricaceæ.		
***Myricaria elegans*, Royle**	**Sat**	**c. 9,000**
	Paipering maidan	**10,990**
Geraniaceæ.		
***Geranium pratense*, L.**	(?)	
***Geranium collinum*, Bieb.**	**Nagyr to Hopar**	**c. 8,500**
Rutaceæ.		
***Ruta Gilesii*, Hemsl. sp. n.**	**Dirran**	**9,500**
Leguminaceæ.		
***Medicago sativa*, L.**	**Nagyr to Hopar**	**c. 8,500**

Name.	Place.	Height in Feet.
Leguminaceæ (*continued*).		
Medicago falcata, L.	Askole	10,360
Medicago lupulina, L.	Nagyr	7,790
	Askole	10,360
Chesneya cuneata, Benth.	Dirran	9,500
Caragana tragacanthoides, Poir. var....	Hatu Pir	c. 10,000
Astragalus adesmiæfolius, Benth. ...	Hunnuno, Hopar	c. 12,000
Astragalus confertus, Benth. ...	Near Strawberry Camp	c. 11,000
	Dasskaram Needle	c. 16,500
Astragalus strictus, Grah.	Burchi	11,080
Astragalus, near *A. oxyodon*, Baker ...	Gargo	11,340
Astragalus frigidus, Benth.	Left moraine, Shallihuru glacier...	c. 13,000
	Left bank, Hispar glacier	c. 12,000
Astragalus Royleanus, Bunge	Sat	c. 9,000
Astragalus sp....	Sat	c. 9,000
Astragalus sp....	Hunnuno, Hopar	c. 12,000
Colutea arborescens, L.	Hispar valley	c. 9,000
Hedysarum Falconeri, Baker ...	Near Strawberry Camp	c. 11,000
	Mir	11,630
Cicer soongarica, Steph.	Burchi	11,080
	Left bank, Hispar glacier	c. 11,000
Sophora alopecuroides, L.	Bagrot valley	c. 8,000
Rosaceæ.		
Cerasus Griffithii, Boiss.	Gilgit Road, Astor to Doian... ...	c. 8,000
Spiræa hypericifolia, L.	Left bank, Hispar glacier	c. 11,000
Fragaria vesca, L....	Burchi	11,080
Potentilla Inglisii, Royle	Dasskaram Needle	c. 17,000
	Snow-lake Camp	16,290
Potentilla fruticosa, L. var. *pumila* ...	Left bank, Hispar glacier	c. 13,500
Potentilla bifurca, L.	Nagyr	7,790
	Hispar	10,320
	Left bank, Hispar glacier	c. 12,000
Potentilla Salessovii, Steph....	Baltoro valley	c. 11,300
Potentilla multifida, L.	Nagyr	7,790
Potentilla desertorum, Bunge ...	Sat	c. 9,000
	Moraine near Gargo	c. 11,500
Potentilla argyrophylla, Wall. ...	Near Strawberry Camp	c. 11,000
	Moraine above Strawberry Camp...	c. 12,000
	Left bank, Shallihuru glacier ...	c. 14,000
Potentilla anserina, L.	Nagyr to Hopar	c. 8,500
Potentilla gelida, C. A. M.	Moraine above Strawberry Camp...	c. 12,000
Potentilla Sibbaldi, Haller f. (*Sibbaldia procumbens*, L.)	Near Strawberry Camp	c. 11,000
Potentilla sericea, L. var.	Left bank, Hispar glacier	c. 12,000
Potentilla, sp....	Nagyr	7,790
Rosa macrophylla, Lindl.	Sat	c. 9,000
	Paipering maidan	10,990
Cotoneaster nummularia, F. and M. ...	Gilgit Road, Astor to Doian	c. 8,000
Saxifragaceæ.		
Ribes himalense, Dcne.	Left bank, Hispar glacier	c. 12,000
Ribes orientale, Poir.	Gilgit Road, Astor to Doian	c. 8,000
Saxifraga sibirica, L.	Moraine above Strawberry Camp...	c. 12,000
Saxifraga flagellaris, Willd.... ...	South slope, Rash ridge	c. 13,000
	Left bank, Hispar glacier	c. 12,000
	Angle of Latok glacier	c. 14,000
Saxifraga imbricata, Royle	Above Trough Camp	c. 16,000
Saxifraga oppositifolia, L.	Dasskaram Needle	17,000
Saxifraga Stracheyi, Hk. f. and T. ...	Hatu Pir	c. 10,000

NAME.	PLACE.	HEIGHT IN FEET.
SAXIFRAGACEÆ (*continued*).		
Saxifraga Hirculus, L.	Skoro La	17,320
Parnassia ovata, Ledeb.	Hopar	9,220
CRASSULACEÆ.		
Sedum tibeticum, Hk. f. and T. ...	Rash ridge	13,400
	Dasskaram Needle	16,500
	Left bank, Hispar glacier	c. 12,000
Sedum Ewersii, Ledeb.	Left bank, Hispar glacier	c. 11,000
	Nambla Brangsa	11,700
	Right bank, Baltoro glacier	c. 14,500
Sedum fastigiatum, Hk. f. and T. ...	Dirran	9,500
Sedum asiaticum, DC.	Moraine above Strawberry Camp...	c. 12,000
	Left moraine, Shallihuru glacier...	c. 13,000
Sempervivum acuminatum, Dcne. ...	Angle of Latok glacier	c. 14,000
Cotyledon leucantha, Ledeb.	Askole to Korofon	c. 10,200
Cotyledon Lievenii, Ledeb.	Hunnuno, Hopar	c. 12,000
HALORAGIDACEÆ.		
Hippuris vulgaris, L.	Barpu	c. 10,000
UMBELLIFERÆ.		
Bupleurum falcatum, L. var. *nigrocarpum*	Shukurri	c. 13,000
Pleurospermum Candollei, Benth. ...	Left bank, Hispar glacier	c. 13,500
Heracleum pinnatum, C. B. Clarke ...	Baltoro valley	c. 11,300
Carum Carui, Linn.	Nagyr	7,790
CAPRIFOLIACEÆ.		
Lonicera glauca, Hk. f. and T.	South slope, Rash ridge	c. 13,000
Lonicera microphylla, Willd.	Paipering maidan	10,990
RUBIACEÆ.		
Galium verum, L.	Left bank, Hispar glacier	c. 11,000
VALERIANACEÆ.		
Valeriana dioica, L.	Hunnuno, Hopar	c. 12,000
	Hatu Pir	c. 10,000
Valeriana Jæschkei, C. B. Clarke ...	Gilgit Road, Astor to Doian	c. 8,000
DIPSACEÆ.		
Morina persica, L.	Laskam slopes...	c. 12,000
COMPOSITÆ.		
Erigeron andryaloides, C. B. Clarke	Near Strawberry Camp	c. 11,000
	Hunnuno, Hopar	c. 12,000
	Barpu	c. 10,000
Erigeron monticolus, DC.	Nagyr	7,790
Erigeron alpinus, L. var. *uniflorus*, Hk. f.	Left bank, Hispar glacier	c. 13,500
Aster tibeticus, Hk. f.	Near Strawberry Camp	c. 11,000
	Hunnuno, Hopar	c. 12,000
Leontopodium alpinum, Cass. ...	Above Trough Camp	c. 16,000
	Hunnuno, Hopar	c. 12,000
	Dasskaram Needle	16,500
	Left bank, Hispar glacier	c. 12,000
Anaphalis virgata, Thoms., and var.	Hunnuno, Hopar	c. 12,000
	The Nose, foot of Biafo glacier ...	c. 10,500
Anaphalis nubigena, DC.	Near Strawberry Camp	c. 11,000
	Mir	11,630

NAME.	PLACE.	HEIGHT IN FEET.
COMPOSITÆ (*continued*).		
Allardia tomentosa, Dcne.	Near Strawberry Camp	c. 11,000
	Left bank, Hispar glacier	c. 12,000
Allardia glabra, Dcne.	Angle of Latok glacier	c. 14,000
Allardia Stoliczkai, C. B. Clarke ...	Near Strawberry Camp	c. 11,000
Allardia nivea, Hk. f. and T.	Baltoro valley	c. 11,300
Tanacetum Senecionis, J. Gay ...	Left bank, Hispar glacier	c. 11,000
	Mango Brangsa	12,600
Artemisia maritima, L....	Hatu Pir	c. 10,000
Artemisia sacrorum, L.	Paipering maidan	10,990
Artemisia, sp.	Askole	10,360
Chrysanthemum Stoliczkai, C. B. Clarke	Left bank, Hispar glacier	c. 11,000
Doronicum Falconeri, C. B. Clarke	Boggy Camp	13,570
	Corner Camp	14,500
Senecio chrysanthemoides, L.	Left bank, Hispar glacier	c. 12,000
Senecio coronopifolius, Desf. ...	Gilgit Road, Astor to Doian	c. 8,000
	Hatu Pir	c. 10,000
Echinops cornigerus, DC.	Near Askole	c. 10,200
Saussurea (?) (no flower)	South slope, Rash ridge	c. 13,000
Cnicus arvensis, Hoffm.	Hispar valley	c. 9,000
Taraxacum officinale, Wigg. var. ...	Left bank, Hispar glacier	c. 13,500
Taraxacum officinale, Wigg. var. ...	Right bank, Biafo glacier	c. 12,500
Crepis flexuosa, C. B. Clarke (*C. glauca*, Bth.)	Near Strawberry Camp	c. 11,000
	Nagyr	7,790
	Left bank, Hispar glacier	c. 11,000
Crepis, sp. (insufficient)	Near Strawberry Camp	c. 11,000
	Nagyr	7,790
Hieracium umbellatum, L. var. *lanceolatum*	Nagyr	7,790
Lactuca dissecta, Don.	Nagyr to Hopar	c. 8,500
Lactuca tatarica, C. A. Mey. ...	Hispar valley	c. 9,000
	Bardumal	11,000
Lactuca decipiens, C. B. Clarke	Baltoro valley	c. 11,300
CAMPANULACEÆ.		
Campanula colorata, Wall.	Nagyr	7,790
	Nagyr to Hopar	c. 8,500
PLUMBAGINACEÆ.		
Acantholimon lycopodioides, Boiss.	Hunnuno, Hopar	c. 12,000
	Korofon	10,360
PRIMULACEÆ.		
Primula farinosa, L. var. *caucasica*, Regel	Near Strawberry Camp	c. 11,000
Primula purpurea, Royle	South slope, Rash ridge	c. 13,000
Glaux maritima, L.	Hopar	9,220
Androsace rotundifolia, Hardw. var. *Thomsoni*, Watt....	Gilgit Road, Astor to Doian	c. 8,000
	Dirran	9,500
Androsace septentrionalis, L. ...	Sat	c. 9,000
	Dirran	9,500
Androsace villosa, L.	Burchi	11,080
	Rash ridge	c. 13,400
GENTIANACEÆ.		
Gentiana squarrosa, Ledeb.	Nagyr	7,790
Gentiana detonsa, Fries.	Nagyr to Hopar	8,500
	Hunnuno, Hopar	c. 12,000
	Mango Brangsa	c. 12,600

Name.	Place.	Height in Feet.
Gentianaceæ (*continued*).		
Gentiana borealis, Bunge	Angle of the Latok glacier	c. 14,000
	Mango Brangsa	12,600
Gentiana carinata, Griseb.	Ogre's Camp	14,230
	Boggy Camp	13,570
Gentiana argentea, Royle	Burchi	11,080
	Mir	11,630
Gentiana tenella, Fries	Corner Camp	14,500
Pleurogyne carinthiaca, Griseb.	Mango Brangsa	12,600
Borraginaceæ.		
Echinospermum barbatum, Lehm.	Rash ridge	c. 13,400
	South slope, Rash ridge	c. 13,000
Bothriospermum sp.	Dirran	9,500
Cynoglossum denticulatum, DC.	Nagyr	7,790
Cynoglossum, sp.	Askole to Korofon	c. 10,200
Eritrichium strictum, Dcne.	Shukurri	c. 13,000
Asperugo procumbens, L.	Gilgit Road, Astor to Doian	c. 8,000
Mertensia primuloides, Benth.	In Sulphur Camp couloir	c. 14,700
	Shukurri	c. 13,000
	Ogre's Camp	14,230
Mertensia echioides, Benth.	Gilgit Road, Astor to Doian	c. 8,000
Arnebia hispidissima, DC.	Baltoro valley	c. 11,300
Macrotomia perennis, Boiss.	Rash ridge	c. 13,400
	Shukurri	c. 13,000
	Left bank, Hispar glacier	c. 12,000
Macrotomia endochroma, Hk. f. and T.	Left bank, Hispar glacier	c. 11,000
Onosma echioides, L.	(?)	
Myosotis sylvatica, Hoffm.	Burchi	11,080
	Nagyr	7,790
Convolvulaceæ.		
Convolvulus arvensis, L.	Nagyr	7,790
Solanaceæ.		
Hyoscyamus niger, L.	Nagyr to Hopar	c. 8,500
Physochlaina prœalta, Hk. f.	Hatu Pir	c. 10,000
Scrophulariaceæ.		
Scrophularia variegata, Bieb.	Dirran	9,500
Veronica biloba, L.	Rash ridge	c. 13,400
Euphrasia officinalis, L.	Barpu	c. 10,000
Pedicularis pectinata, Wall.	Left bank, Hispar glacier	c. 12,000
Pedicularis pycnantha, Boiss.	Rash ridge	c. 13,400
	South slope, Rash ridge	c. 13,000
Orobanchaceæ.		
Orobanche indica, Ham.	Laskam slopes	c. 12,000
Orobanche Hansii, Kerner (?)	Korofon	10,360
Labiatæ.		
Plectranthus rugosus, Wall.	Nagyr to Hopar	c. 8,500
Thymus Serpyllum, L.	Near Strawberry Camp	c. 11,000
	Rash ridge	c. 13,400
	Mir	11,630
Dracocephalum nutans, L.	Moraine above Strawberry Camp	c. 12,000
Dracocephalum, near *D. palmatum*, Steph.	Rash ridge	c. 13,400
Stachys tibetica, Vatke	Nagyr to Hopar	c. 8,500
Stachys tibetica, Vatke, var. *pinnatifida*, Hemsl.	Nagyr	7,790

NAME.	PLACE.	HEIGHT IN FEET.
LABIATÆ (*continued*).		
Nepeta discolor, Royle	Left bank, Hispar glacier	c. 11,000
POLYGONACEÆ.		
Polygonum viviparum, L. var. ...	Burchi	11,080
	Left bank, Hispar glacier	c. 13,500
	Boggy Camp	13,570
Polygonum affine, Don.	Near Strawberry Camp	c. 11,000
	Mir	11,630
Oxyria digyna, Hill	Near Strawberry Camp	c. 11,000
Fagopyrum tataricum, Gærtn.	Askole	10,360
CHENOPODIACEÆ.		
Eurotia ceratoides, C. A. M. ♂	Baltoro valley	c. 11,300
Atriplex, sp.	Askole	10,360
THYMELÆACEÆ.		
Daphne oleoides, Schreb.	Sat	c. 9,000
ELÆAGNACEÆ.		
Hippophaë rhamnoides, L.	Baltoro valley	c. 11,300
SANTALACEÆ.		
Thesium himalense, Royle	South slope, Rash ridge	c. 13,000
SALICACEÆ.		
Salix...	Dirran	9,500
Salix, near *S. flabellaris*, Anders. ...	Mango Brangsa	12,600
Salix oxycarpa, Anders. (?)...	Paipering maidan	10,990
Salix hastata, L.	Left bank, Hispar glacier	c. 12,000
GNETACEÆ.		
Ephedra monosperma, C. A. M.	Korofon	10,360
Ephedra monosperma, C. A. M., an *E. Gerrardiana*, Wall. var. *Wallichiana*, Stapf (?)...	Rash ridge	c. 13,400
CONIFERÆ.		
Juniperus pseudosabina, F. and M. ...	South slope, Rash ridge	c. 13,000
ORCHIDACEÆ.		
Orchis latifolia, L....	Nagyr to Hopar	c. 8,500
	Barpu	c. 10,000
LILIACEÆ.		
Tulipa chrysantha, Boiss.	Gilgit Road, Astor to Doian	c. 8,000
Lloydia serotina, Rchb.	Left bank, Hispar glacier	c. 13,000
Gagea lutea, Ker.	Dirran	9,500
Allium senescens, L. var.	Baltoro valley	c. 11,300
Allium blandum, Wall.	Mango Brangsa	12,600
JUNCACEÆ.		
Juncus membranaceus, F. Buchen.	Left bank, Hispar glacier	c. 11,000
	Left bank, Hispar glacier	c. 12,000
NAIADACEÆ.		
Potamogeton pectinatus, L.	Mir	11,630
CYPERACEÆ.		
Carex Moorcroftii, Boott	Left bank, Hispar glacier	c. 13,000

NAME.	PLACE.	HEIGHT IN FEET.
GRAMINEÆ.		
Phragmites communis, L.	Hispar valley	c. 9,000
MUSCI.		
Bryum cæspiticium, L.	Left bank, Hispar glacier	c. 12,000
Polytrichum, sp.	Sat	c. 9,000
Barbula rigida, Schultz	Surface of the Baltoro glacier ...	c. 15,000

BUTTERFLIES.

BUTTERFLIES.

By Mr. W. F. Kirby, F.L.S., F.E.S., Assistant in the Zoological Department, British Museum (Natural History), South Kensington.

NYMPHALIDÆ.

Satyrinæ.

Erebia mani, De Nicéville (Baltoro glacier, c. 14,000 ft.).

A rare species in collections; originally described from Ladak.

Amecera menava, Moore (Samaiyar valley, c. 10,000 ft.).

Common in the Western Himalayas, and met with in Beluchistan. If the Russian authors have correctly identified this species, it is found along the mountain ranges of Central Asia as far as Transcaucasia. It is allied to our European Wall Brown butterflies, *A. mæra* and *A. megæra.*

Epinephile pulchella, Felder (Mouth of Punmah valley, c. 10,500 ft.).

Small specimens, not measuring more than an inch and a quarter across the wings. Found at a great elevation in the Western Himalayas, Spiti, Ladak, and Central Asia. It somewhat resembles our Meadow Brown and Large Heath butterflies (*E. janira* and *E. tithonus*), which belong to the same genus.

Hipparchia lehana, Moore (Askole and Mouth of Punmah valley, 10,000–12,000 ft.).

Found in the mountains of Ladak and Central Asia. It belongs to the typical group of the genus which is most richly represented in Eastern Europe and Western Asia.

Hipparchia heydenreichii, Lederer (Mangjong, c. 11,500 ft.).

A mountain species, found in Central Asia from the Altai to Kashmir. It is allied to the European *H. briseis.*

Hipparchia parisatis, Kollar (Skardo, c. 7,000 ft.).

A handsome dark species with a bluish-white border, common from Armenia to the Himalayas.

Nymphalinæ.

Argynnis vitatha, Moore (Mir, 11,630 ft.).

A scarce insect in collections; described from Kashmir. It is closely allied to the common European Dark Green Fritillary (*A. aglaia*, Linn.), with which Groum-Grshimailo considers it identical.

Argynnis jerdoni, Lang (Mir, 11,630 ft.).

Argynnis sipura, Moore (Boggy Camp, 13,570 ft.).

Two little-known Kashmir species, genuine mountain species allied to some of the smaller Fritillaries found in the European Alps.

Pyrameis cardui, Linn. (Hunza, Nagyr, Hopar, 7,000–9,000 ft.).

Our common Painted Lady butterfly, an almost cosmopolitan species.

LYCÆNIDÆ.

Chrysophanus phlœas, Linn. var. *timeus*, Cramer.*

A dark variety of our common Small Copper butterfly, which is found, with slight variations, throughout the greater part of Europe and Asia.

Polyommatus, sp. near *argus*, Linn. (Nagyr, c. 7,000 ft.).

Polyommatus, sp. near *hylas*, Denis.*

These two species I cannot at present determine.

Polyommatus pheretes, Hübner, var. *asiatica*, Elwes.

Found in Sikkim and Kashmir; the Indian form of a well-known butterfly found at a high elevation in the Swiss Alps.

Polyommatus ariana, Moore (Bulchi, 11,080 ft.; Baltoro glacier, c. 14,000 ft.).

Common in the mountains of North India; allied to the European and Asiatic *P. icarus*, Rottenburg.

Polyommatus amphissa, Moore (Mir, 11,630 ft.; Rash ridge, c. 12,500 ft.; Baltoro glacier, c. 14,000 ft.).

A species only recorded from Ladak. The hind wings are green beneath, as in the European *P. cyllarus*, Rottenburg.

PAPILIONIDÆ.

Pierinæ.

Pieris brassicæ, Linn. var. *nipalensis*, Gray (Nagyr, 6,500–8,000 ft.).

The well-known Himalayan form of our common Large White Cabbage butterfly.

Pieris rapæ, Linn. var. *mannii*, Mayer (Bulchi, 8,110 ft.).

Agrees best with the form of our Small White Cabbage butterfly, which is found in Dalmatia, Turkey, &c.

Pieris daplidice, Linn. var. (Nagyr, c. 7,500 ft.).

A rather brightly coloured form of our Bath White butterfly.

Pieris callidice, Esper (Samaiyar glacier, c. 14,000 ft.; Mir, 11,630 ft.; Rash ridge, c. 12,500 ft.; Baltoro glacier, c. 13,000 ft.).

A common mountain butterfly in Europe and Asia.†

Colias erate, Esper (above Mangjong, c. 12,000 ft.).

A species met with from South Russia throughout Asia to the Amur and North India.

Colias hyale, Linn. (? ?) var. *sareptensis*, Standinger.*

The form of our Pale Clouded Yellow which is commonest in South Russia and Western Asia. I may here express my opinion that the true *C. hyale*, Linn. is the female of *C. edusa*, Fabricius.

---

* The label of this fell off and was lost on the journey. The butterfly was found in the neighbourhood of Askole.

† This was the commonest butterfly we met with at high altitudes; we saw it, I believe, up to at least 16,000 ft., and on all the glaciers we went up.—W. M. C.

Colias eogene, Felder (Hispar glacier, c. 13,500 ft.; Baltoro glacier, c. 12,500 ft.).

A very deeply coloured species, at present rather scarce in collections. It occurs in Kashmir, the Hindu Kush, and the Pamirs.

PAPILIONINÆ.

Parnassius intermedius, Ménétriès (Askole, 10,360 ft.).

This insect, which many authors regard as a local form of the European *P. delius*. Esper, is found throughout Southern Siberia and the western part of Central Asia.

HESPERIIDÆ.

Hesperia andromedæ, Wallengren (Mir, 11,630 ft.).

A species widely distributed in the mountains of Europe.

MOTHS.

MOTHS.

Named by Dr. A. G. Butler, F.L.S., F.Z.S., &c., Assistant Keeper in the Zoological Department, British Museum (Natural History), South Kensington.

Noctuites.

Agrotis ypsilon, Rott. (Nagyr, 7,790 ft.).

Heliothis dipsacea, Linn. (Baltit, 7,940 ft.).

Two widely distributed British species.

Dianthœcia christophi, Möschl. (label lost).

A South Russian species.

Geometrites.

Stamnodes pauperaria, Everson (Gandar, 13,070 ft.).

Nemoria gelida, Butler (Hopar, 9,220 ft.).

A rare species belonging to a well-known European genus of green moths.

Pyralites.

Phlyctenodes comparalis, Hübner (Bulchi, 8,110 ft.).

Spilodes verticalis, Linn. (Baltoro glacier, 14,100 ft.).

A widely distributed British species.

DESCRIPTION OF TWO SKULLS BROUGHT BY MR. CONWAY FROM NAGYR.

DESCRIPTION OF TWO SKULLS BROUGHT BY MR. CONWAY FROM NAGYR.

By W. LAURENCE H. DUCKWORTH, B.A., Scholar of Jesus College, Cambridge.

To the Cambridge University Collection there have recently been added two skulls from the capital of Nagyr, a small state in Central Asia. By the kindness of Prof. Macalister I am enabled to give the following description of them :—

The skulls are numbered 1204 and 1205 respectively, in the Cambridge catalogue ; the measurements, which were made with Flower's Craniometer and a steel tape, are given in millimetres.

The skull 1204 is a female skull whose sex is indicated by an inconspicuous glabella, faintly defined superciliary ridges, temporal ridges and external occipital protuberance, slender zygomatic arches. It is in a good state of preservation, the left side being a good deal more bleached than the right ; no remains of skin or adhering hairs are to be seen. The more conspicuous parts missing are as follows :—The lower jaw, all the teeth except four (first and second molars on either side), the lachrymal bones, the hamular processes of the internal pterygoid plates, the left styloid process (that on the right side, though quite short (8 mm.), does not appear to have been broken off). The os planum of the ethmoid is much damaged on either side.

This skull is fairly symmetrical ; the right parietal eminence is the more pronounced ; on the left side is a parietal foramen.

At the right asterion are three large wormian bones, and at the left asterion a single one. The temporal ridge of the right side is more pronounced than that on the left (and the remaining molar teeth of the right side have larger dimensions than those on the left). There is a post-condylar foramen of large size on the right side, in front of and external to which is a remarkable eminence perforated at the top where the bone is thinned out. This is due to pressure of the right sigmoid sinus causing absorption of the bone and consequent dilatation of the sinus in this region (just before its termination). The anterior condylar foramina are large, but neither is subdivided. The foramen spinosum is incomplete on either side, but this is possibly due to injury. The nasal bones are curiously asymmetrical. The suture between them is oblique in direction, and at its highest point is 3 mm. to the left of the remaining trace of the metopic suture, whereas its lower end reaches to the middle line of the face; the width of the nasal bones at their upper ends varies correspondingly, for the right nasal bone is 6 mm. and the left 4 mm. wide at this end. The anterior opening of the nose is also asymmetrical, the right superior maxillary bone being hollowed out to a much deeper level than is the left; the septum of the nose is strongly deflected to the left.

The dentition has been perfect. The premaxillo-maxillary suture is still visible; the sagittal suture shows no signs of synostosis, nor has the spheno-basilar suture yet synostosed. These facts assign an age of from 18 to 21 years to this skull.

The general shape and contours are of a refined type, the forehead being high, no prominent glabella, distinct frontal eminences with a slight flattening immediately posterior to these. The curve of the vault reaches its culminating point just at the bregma, and begins to descend some 40 mm. posterior to this point. From the obelion, the posterior curve continues to the lambda, after passing which it is interrupted by a considerable bulging out in the region immediately above the inion.

In norma verticalis the skull is seen to be cryptozygous and dolichocephalic. The breadth-index, 69·94, is remarkably low. There is a depression at the level of the upper part of the temporal ridge, below each parietal eminence, below which again is an eminence above the mastoid process, and it is at this level that the breadth of the skull is greatest. The transverse arc is quite regular, no flattening or upraising at the vertex. The mastoid processes are small, in fact feminine, and the same description applies to the face generally.

The coronal, sagittal, and lambdoid sutures are of moderate complexity. In the coronal suture just above the left stephanion appear the remains of a wormian bone, interrupting the suture for some 15 mm.; ossification has taken place around the circumference for about half its extent. The sagittal suture becomes more simple for a space of 25 mm. in the region of the obelion. The lambdoidal suture is characterised by the wormian bones already referred to. On the right side there is a large foramen in one wormian bone and another in the base of the mastoid process.

On the left side are two foramina near the base of the mastoid process, formed by the juxtaposition of notches in the borders of the temporal and occipital bones respectively. The metopic suture persists for a distance of 2 mm. only.

This skull weighs 419 gms.; decidedly light. The cranial capacity (using No. 8 shot) is 1470 c.c., an exceptionally high figure for a female skull. As regards the face, the orbits are mesoseme, and droop slightly and externally; there are shallow supra-orbital notches. The nose is mesorrhine and the lower margins of its anterior opening are rounded; the spine is small and the profile outline is nearly straight. There is a well-marked depression immediately below the infra-orbital foramen. The palate is distinctly elliptical, of no great depth; the posterior nares are small. The occipital condyles are small, their inner and anterior lips are prominent and not much elevated above the plane of the foramen magnum.

An internal occipital protuberance can be felt, and the torcular herophili seems to have been situated on its left side.

Turning now to the skull No. 1205, a series of contrasts present themselves. No. 1205 is a male skull—the prominent glabella, superciliary ridges, occipital protuberance, and mastoid processes, as well as the stoutness of the zygoma, indicate this. It is not in so good a state of preservation as is No. 1204, and the following parts are wanting:—The lower jaw, styloid processes, right internal pterygoid plate, left hamular process, left inferior turbinated bone, the posterior part of the vomer and the left lachrymal bone. Three teeth alone remain, and the alveolar arch has undergone a considerable amount of absorption.

The most striking features are: the rough and uneven surface; very marked dolichocephaly (index 68·28), considerable flattening in the region of the obelion, where there are two parietal foramina; the skull is also slightly plagiocephalic. There are two wormian bones on the right side below the asterion. The appearance of the condyles is noticeable. The left condyle is subdivided by a somewhat oblique sulcus so as to present two oval articular areas. The articular surface of the right condyle is constricted, at about the same level, but is not completely interrupted.

There is a post-condylar foramen on the right side. The outer pterygoid plates are much everted, and on the left side a bridge of bone connects the base of the external pterygoid plate with the base of the spine of the sphenoid. This is the superior variety of the pterygo-spinous ligament ossified. On the right side a depression exists immediately external to the external pterygoid plate.

The age of this skull is not very closely indicated. The third molars on either side have been lost and their alveoli closed, and since ossification is just commencing in the sagittal suture in the region of the obelion, it may be assumed that the person had passed middle age. The general contour is characterised by the very prominent glabella, with a depression immediately above it; the curve of the vault reaches its maximum about 25 mm. posterior to the bregma; and the region of the obelion is much flattened, as has been already remarked. Beyond the lambda there is a considerable bulging out of the occipital bone, reduced at the occipital protuberance, whence a well-marked occipital crest descends to the opisthion. Altogether this contour is somewhat irregular, contrasting strongly with that of No. 1204.

On a horizontal plane, *i.e.*, in norma verticalis, the skull is seen to be phænozygous, and its left side is somewhat flattened. The transverse arc in the region of the coronal suture is quite regular. Posterior to this, the highest point of the arc is seen to be at a distance of 17 mm. to the left of the middle line; still more posteriorily this arc is interrupted by the flattening in the region of the obelion.

The sutures are moderately complex. The outline of the squamous portion of the left temporal bone overlapping the parietal bone is noticeable, as it culminates in a sharp spine vertically above the external auditory meatus; on the right side the outline of the corresponding suture is more regular. The remaining teeth are of large size, and show signs of having been well used. The cranial capacity, 1375 c.c., and the weight, 667 gms., afford contrasts with the skull No. 1204.

The orbits are mesoseme, though their respective indices differ considerably; there is a supra-orbital notch on the right side and a supra-orbital foramen on the left side. The lower margins of the anterior nares are rounded; the nose is mesorrhine, inclined to the leptorrhine type; the nasal spine is large. The alveolar index shows that the skull is orthognathic, but is not reliable owing to the absorption of the alveolar arch, the effect of which, aggravated by the length of time that has elapsed since the skull was interred, is to reduce the basi-alveolar length. The palate seems to have been elliptical. Traces of a premaxillo-maxillary suture remain, but these are lost near the middle line of the palate.

There is a somewhat large foramen in the basi-occipital on the lip of the foramen magnum, midway between the condyles, corresponding to the attachment of the suspensory ligament of the odontoid process of the axis. The internal occipital protuberance corresponds in position with the external, and the torcular herophili was situated on the right side of this point.

Such are the characters of the two skulls. The contrasts between them arise rather from differences of sex and age than from any other causes. Their type is Caucasian, in spite of the low figures representing their respective cephalic indices. There may be compared with them the following examples (figures in brackets refer to the list of authors) :—

First, the series of skulls from the Hindu-Kush, described by Dr. Garson in 1888. (i.) These came from localities at distances from Nagyr of thirty to one hundred miles. Of the five skulls two are dolichocephalic, the remainder are mesaticephalic; the most dolichocephalic had a breadth index of 72·3, and a general comparison of their measurements with those of the two Nagyr specimens brings to light a general resemblance.*

Secondly, there are two skulls from Srinagar (the capital of Kashmir), briefly described by Capt. Cunningham (ii.) in 1854. Sketches of the two skulls (a male and a female) are given, and the difference between these skulls and the shorter skulls with wider zygomatic arches of tribes more Mongolian in type is noticed. No measurements, however, are given. From the sketches, a general resemblance to the Nagyr skull is apparent, more particularly as regards the shape of the palate in the female skull. The same sketches are referred to in the "Crania Ethnica" of Quatrefages and Hamy.

In the third place, are the skulls presented to the Société Anthropologique de Paris by M. de Ujfalvy in 1882 (iii.); they are described as having been obtained from a Mussulman cemetery in Kashmir. A committee was appointed to examine and report on the skulls, but so far no report has been available.

Turning to measurements on living persons, there may be mentioned M. de Ujfalvy's account of a native of Hunza whom he measured. (iv.) This man was dolichocephalic with a cephalic index of 73·84. To obtain the corresponding index for the skull itself, two units should be subtracted according to Broca ("Bull. Soc. d'Anthrop.," 2nd series, vol. iii., 1868). The resulting index of 71·84 is quite comparable with the foregoing

* Dr. Garson has remarked on the prominent brow-ridges common to the Nagyr skull, No. 1205, and to the Hindu-Kush skulls, also on approximation of the cranial capacity in one case.

instances. M. de Ujfalvy at the same time took measurements of a native of Naghar (? Nagyr), but these were not placed on record in the Society's report.

Such are the cases for direct comparison. On looking through the catalogue of the museum of the Royal College of Surgeons, the following crania from Hindustan seemed to present points of similarity to those from Nagyr, viz., Nos. 632, 634, and 670; their measurements have been tabulated with those of the Nagyr skulls (Table II.).

A comparison has been instituted between the measurements of the Nagyr skulls on the one hand, of those of various natives of Ceylon on the other. A general review of the figures shows that the two Nagyr skulls resemble each other more closely than any of the skulls compared with them (see Tables III. or IV.); the most interesting comparison is afforded by the data for the Rhodias of Ceylon (presumably the Rodiya mentioned by Dr. Hyde Clarke) (xviii.).

TABLE I.

MEASUREMENTS OF THE SKULLS ARE IN MILLIMETRES.

INDICES.	Skull, ♀ Nagyr, 1204.	Skull, ♂ Nagyr, 1205.
(Bi) Cephalic	69·94	68·28
(Hi Vertical	69·94	70·43
(Ai) Alveolar	95 ?	97·10 ?
(Oi) Orbital	86·48 (R)	82·06 (R)
(Ni) Nasal	50	52·72
Stephano-zygomatic	97·5	82·4
Palatine	115·4	...
Naso-malar	110·50	113·33

CRANIAL CAPACITY.	1470 c.c.	1375 c.c.
Maximum Antero-posterior Length...	183	186
Maximum Transverse Diameter	128	127
Basi-alveolar Length	95 ?	101 ?
Basi-nasal Length	100	104
Basi-bregmatic Length	128	131
Length: Basion to Inion	63	87
" " Opisthion	31	38
" Opisthion to Glabella	137 ?	144
" Nasi-alveolar	60	75 ?
" of Spheno-parietal suture...	10	15 R 17 L

TABLE I.—(*Continued.*)

MEASUREMENTS OF THE SKULL ARE IN MILLIMETRES.

CRANIAL CAPACITY.	1470 c. c.	1375 c.c.
Breadth of Foramen magnum	27	29
„ from Pterion to Pterion	104	112
„ from Stephanion to Stephanion	117	103
„ from Asterion to Asterion	105	104
„ Bizygomatic	120	125
„ Bi-maxillary	89	96
„ Interauricular	107	113
„ Minimum Interorbital	19	22
„ Minimum Frontal	101	95
„ Bi-orbital (at Fronto-malar suture)	102	101
Orbital Breadth	37	39
Orbital Height	32	32
Nasal Breadth	22	29
Nasal Height	44	55
Maximum Length of the Palate	52	57 ?
Maximum Breadth „ outside arch	60	64
„ „ „ inside arch	42	45 ?
Arcs :—		
Antero-posterior curve. Frontal arc	129	123
Parietal arc	125	122
Arc from Lambda to Inion	88	65
„ Inion to Basion	63	94
„ Inion to Opisthion	32	55
Supra-auricular arc	302	307
Jugo-nasal arc	105	110
Breadth at external border of Orbits for Naso-malar Index	95	98
Horizontal circumference	508	507
Posterior Nares—		
Maximum Breadth (between Intl. Pterygoid plates)...	27	30
Height	23	23
Length of Interpalatine suture	14	17
The Superior Maxillary Bone—		
Maximum Height	57	72 ?
Mean Height	35	47
Minimum Height...	17	23

DIMENSIONS OF TEETH. Skull, ♀ Nagyr, 1204.

	Antero-posterior diameter.	Transverse diameter.
On the Right—		
Molar 1	10	11
Molar 2	9	10
On the Left—		
Molar 1	7	10
Molar 2	8	8

TABLE I.—(*Continued.*)

Skull, ♂ Nagyr, 1205.

	Antero-posterior diameter.	Transverse diameter.
On the Left Side—		
2nd Premolar ...	7	8
1st Molar	11	11
2nd Molar	10	10

TABLE II.

COMPARISON OF MEASUREMENTS OF SKULLS FROM NAGYR with those of Skulls from the Hindu-Kush described by Dr. Garson (i.) and with isolated examples of Dolichocephalic Skulls which were obtained from other parts of Hindustan.

Skull.	Horizontal circumference.	Maximum Length.	Maximum Breadth.	Breadth Index.	Height.	Height Index.
Nagyr (1204)...	508	183	128	69·94	128	69·94
Nagyr (1205)...	507	186	127	68·28	131	70·43
Gound:						
No. 634 in the catalogue of the Roy. Coll. Surgeons	505	188	127	67·6	134	71·3
Hindu-Kush B	515	181	136	75·1	128	70·7
" C	483	177	128	72·3	123	69·5
" D	500	178	134	75·8	129	72·5
" E	508	176	140	79·5	127	72·1
" F	490?	179	133	74·3	128	71·5
M. de Ujfalvy's Hunza (iv.)	?	?	?	73·84 (71·84)	?	?
Skull from Madura, 670 in catalogue of Roy. Coll. Surgeons	507	184	124	67·4	143	77·7
Skull of a Mussulman, 632 in catalogue of Roy. Coll. Surgeons	512	189	125	66·1	132	69·8

TABLE III.

COMPARISONS OF MEASUREMENTS OF NAGYR SKULLS with those of Living Rhodias.

Skull.	Craniometric.		Anthropometric.	
	Nagyr, 1204 (female).	Nagyr, 1205 (male).	Rhodia (male).	Rhodia (female).
Antero-posterior diameter ...	183	186	190·66 (6)	181·66 (6)
Maximum transverse diameter ...	128	127	139·5 (6)	137·81 (6)
Cephalic Index	69·94	68·28	73·16	75·86
Horizontal circumference	508	507	541·16 (6)	544·66 (6)
Minimum frontal breadth ...	101	95	106·16 (6)	94·83 (6)
Bizgomatic breadth	120	125	120 (12)	
Bi-auricular breadth	107	113	117 (12)	
External Bi-orbital breadth ...	95	98	98·66	

The above measurements of Rhodias are given by M. Emile Deschamps in his account of "Les Veddas de Ceylan," in "L'Anthropologie" for 1891; photographs of male and female Rhodias are also given; in the profile view of a Rhodia chief, the brow presents the same feature of prominent glabella with a depression immediately above it, as does the male skull from Nagyr. The figures in the table above, when allowance is made for the difference between Anthropometric and Craniometric observations, afford some interesting comparisons, those of the respective horizontal circumferences being remarkable. Topinard (xxv.) states that for a skull with a circumference of 508 mm. (horizontal) there should be added 35 mm. to approximate to the corresponding Anthropometric measurement. In the case of Nagyr, 1204, this would give 543 mm., and for Nagyr, 1205, the anthropometric equivalent would be 542 mm.

TABLE IV.

COMPARISON OF MEASUREMENTS OF SKULLS FROM NAGYR with those of Skulls of Natives of Ceylon other than Rhodias.

Skull.	Nagyr, 1204 ♀.	Nagyr, 1205 ♂.	Veddah ♂.	Veddah ♀.	Tamil ♂.
Capacity	1470	1375	1277 (22)	1139 (10)	1336 (13)
Height Index	69·94	70·43	73·8 (21)	73·2 (10)	73·6 (13)
Basi-Nasal Length	100	104	98·7 (18)	93·4 (8)	102·5 (13)
Basi-Alveolar Length	95	101 ?	94·2 (16)	88·3 (8)	99·7 (10)
Alveolar Index	95	97·10	95·2 (16)	94·5 (8)	97·7 (10)
Orbital Index	86·43	82·06	89·2 (21)	89·4 (10)	86·7 (10)
Interorbital breadth	19	22	22·2 (21)	21·7 (10)	23·5 (13)
Nasal Index	50	52·72	52·5 (21)	52 (8)	53·7 (13)
Cephalic Index	69·94	68·28	71·6 (21)	71·2 (11)	70·8 (13)

The measurements of the Veddah and Tamil skulls are those given by Drs. Paul and Fritz Sarasin (xxiv.). The numbers in brackets indicate the number of skulls whence the average is deduced.

Dr. Deniker has most kindly communicated detailed measurements of the series of skulls of Kashmiris, presented to the Société Anthropologique de Paris by M. de Ujfalvy. The series comprises six skulls of males and three of females. Apart from measurements, Dr. Deniker says that the prominence of the inferior nasal spine and the shape of the apertura pyriformis of the nose (that of an ace of hearts) are characteristic of this series. For the measurements, the following arrangement exhibits the principal features, with which those of the skulls from Nagyr may be compared :—

Skull.	Breadth Index.	Height Index.	Nasal Index.
Nagyr, 1205	63·28	70·43	52·7
Average of five male skulls from Kashmir	73·28	70·7	48·3
Extremes	75·6	73·4	54·7
	70·6	65·8	41·5
Kashmir skull, No. 9 (male)	65·6	67·2	?

No. 9 is described separately, as Dr. Deniker suspects deformity.

Female Skulls.

Skull.	Breadth Index.	Height Index.	Nasal Index.
Nagyr, No. 1204	69·94	69·94	50
Kashmir, No. 5	72·3	74·7	51·1
„ No. 6	74	70·7	43·8
„ No. 4 (Child ?)	75·9	77·7	54·5

The conclusion is, that the skulls from Nagyr might well fall into a group including these skulls from Kashmir, except as regards their breadth-index, though even this pronounced feature is surpassed by one of the Kashmir skulls. It seems probable that this may prove to be a specific distinction of skulls from Hunza-Nagyr.

References.

i. Dr. J. G. Garson. "Journal of the Anthropological Institute." Vol. XVIII. 1889.

ii. Capt. Cunningham. "Ladakh and the Surrounding Countries." 1854.

iii. M. de Ujfalvy. "Bulletin de la Société Anthropologique de Paris," 3e Série, Tome V. 1882. p. 212.
iv. M. de Ujfalvy. "Bulletin de la Société Anthropologique de Paris," 1881. p. 600.
v. Vigne. "Travels," 1842. Vol. II. p. 288.
vi. Dr. G. W. Leitner. "Journal of the Anthropological Society." Meeting of Nov. 30th, 1869.
vii. Dr. G. W. Leitner. "Indian Antiquary." Jan. 5th, 1872. p. 8.
viii. Dr. G. W. Leitner. "Report of the British Association." 1875. p. 176.
ix. Dr. G. W. Leitner. "Asiatic Quarterly Review." New Series. Vol. II. July, October, 1891. pp. 139, 204, 243.
x. Dr. G. W. Leitner. "Asiatic Quarterly Review." New Series. Vol. III. January, April, 1892. p. 53.
xi. Drew (F.). "British Association Report." 1874. p. 149.
xii. Drew (F.). "Northern Barrier of India." 1877. p. 167.
xiii. Gen. Maclagan. "Encyclopædia Britannica." Article "Kashmir."
xiv. Lieut. Gordon. "The Roof of the World." 1876. p. 139.
xv. "Archiv für Anthropologie." Vieweg u. Sohn Braunschweig. Band 17. 1887.
xvi. W. W. Hunter. "Imperial Gazetteer of India." 1886. Vol. V. Article "Gilghit."
xvii. Dr. G. Capus. "Revue Scientifique." IIIe Série. Tome XVII. Jan. to July, 1889. p. 7.
xviii. Dr. Hyde Clarke. "Indian Antiquary," 1872. August 2nd.
xix. Col. Biddulph. "Journal of the Royal Asiatic Society." Vol. XVII. New Series. 1885.
xx. M. de Ujfalvy. "Bulletin de la Société Anthropologique de Paris." Séance du 16 Mars, 1882. p. 226.
xxi. Prof. E. E. Oliver. "Pathan and Biloch." 1890. pp. 320–327.
xxii. E. F. Knight. "Where Three Empires Meet." 1893. (Longmans.)
xxiii. Emile Deschamps. "Les Veddas de Ceylan." L'Anthropologie. 1891.
xxiv. Paul and Fritz Sarasin. "Ergebnisse Naturwissenschaftlicher forschungen auf Ceylon." 1893.
xxv. Dr. P. Topinard. "Eléments d'Anthropologie Générale." 1885. p. 711.
xxvi. Biddulph. "Races of the Hindu-Kush."

MOUNTAIN SICKNESS.

MOUNTAIN SICKNESS.

BASED ON NOTES BY MR. W. M. CONWAY, OF HIS EXPERIENCES IN THE KARAKORAM-HIMALAYAS.

WHEN, in mountain climbing, a height of 16,000 to 17,000 feet is reached, the generality of people experience, to a greater or less degree, a train of symptoms to which the term mountain sickness (Fr. *mal des montagnes;* Ger. *Bergkrankheit*) is applied. These symptoms become more and more distressing the more the above heights are exceeded, without however varying in kind, and may become so serious that the life of the individual is endangered. There is still a good deal that is obscure about the condition, therefore the observations made by Conway, who with his guides has climbed higher than any previous traveller, and who seems a very good observer, are of interest and importance. When he left England for his expedition in the Karakoram district he took with him, at Clifford Allbutt's suggestion, a Dudgeon's sphygmograph with which he took pulse curves at different heights up to 23,000 feet, from himself and other members of his expedition. Some of these tracings were lost in transmission to England, but enough remain to teach all that we can expect to learn from such records. These curves he has placed in my hands for examination, and I will presently reproduce some of the more important of them, and draw such conclusions as they seem to allow of.

On Conway's return to England I asked him to write out

his notes on the effects of height, and let me have them along with the pulse curves. I here insert these notes :—

General Notes by W. M. Conway.

" *Vomiting.*—We had only two cases of this—both Gurkhas; one at Footstool Camp (about 17,000 feet), the other on the Pioneer Peak, where Amar Sing had to stop at 22,000 feet, on the Water Col (*see* No. 11). The Gurkha ill at Footstool Camp was a youth. The Gurkhas, for *caste* reasons, had to eat their ordinary food everywhere. We changed our food as we went higher, and on the actual ascent of big peaks only ate Kola biscuits after leaving camp and before getting back to it again. I ascribe our freedom from indigestion to this precaution.

" As to our general experiences I may note as follows :—

" The effect of altitude came upon us all quite gradually, and appeared to affect the native coolies (born and bred at 10,000 feet) as much as ourselves. There were slight individual differences between us, but nothing at all marked. The way altitude showed itself was by our diminished pace when we thought we were going as fast as at lower levels. Referring to our ascent from Asholey to Baltoro, then up the Baltoro glacier to Junction Camp, Footstool Camp, and so to the top of the Pioneer Peak (23,000 feet), descending to Footstool Camp and then down the Baltoro glacier again to Corner Camp, Baltoro and Asholey, I note that we first became definitely conscious of discomfort between Junction Camp (16,000 feet) and Footstool Camp (17,000 feet)—a very gentle slope. I halted at Junction Camp; Bruce and Zurbriggen went on to Footstool Camp, and it was there that the young Gurkha was sick and generally upset. Bad weather came on, and Bruce and Zurbriggen returned to Junction Camp and warned us that we should feel the altitude a short way further up. I stayed four days at Junction Camp and then followed Bruce and Zurbriggen to Footstool Camp. I ought to have been habituated to altitude by then, but was not, and felt exactly as Bruce and Zurbriggen had felt both times they passed that way. This part of the glacier was a straight, almost level, trough between two high walls of mountains right and left. Above Footstool Camp the ascent was through a difficult ice-fall. Here, when we got into enclosed places, with the sun hot on us, we felt altitude badly, when in shady places less, and in general when the sun was hot on us we always felt worse than when it was shut off by clouds, rocks, or ice. There was, as we ascended, a steady diminution in our powers, a desire to keep the arms from hanging by our sides, a disinclination to start observing instruments or doing anything. We had to breathe steadily, the least holding of the breath (to observe an instrument, or take a long stride) being instantly punished by giddiness and puffing. The higher we got the more conscious were we of our hearts—unable to sleep on our left sides, tendency to palpitation even at night. Our feet easily and rapidly got cold and lost sensation. By night we were always more comfortable than by day, and in cloudy than in fine weather. We could have done much more by night if our feet had been able to hold out against the cold. On the peak we felt much worse on slopes than on the arête; we had difficulty to restrain ourselves from taking to the *cornice.* We often felt in hollow places and even on slopes the sensation as through the air was *stagnant.* The night at the highest camp *after* the ascent of Pioneer Peak was our worst night; palpitations constantly woke me up. In the descent we felt discomfort (such as was experienced in the ascent between Junction and Footstool Camps) down to a much lower level, as far as Corner Camp (13,000 feet), than we had felt in the ascent. We seemed to become continuously *less* able to hold out against altitude the longer we remained at a high level. I several times took my temperature, but never hit it at anything but normal. I did not take it on Pioneer Peak. I have said that I thought our appetites remained as usual. I think that I was in error. We did not eat so much at the two highest camps, but we should have eaten more than we did if we had had more to eat. I cannot say how we should have been affected in the latter case."

The ages of the European members of the party were—W. M. Conway, 36; M. Zurbriggen, 34; J. McCormick, 33; J. H. Roudebush, 21; O. Eckenstein, 34.

With regard to the height at which distinct symptoms first show themselves, Conway's account agrees very well with the experiences of the Schlagintweits,[1] who had very extended experience and moved with fairly large parties of natives among the Himalaya, Karakoram, and Kuenluen districts, and who noted that "for the generality of people the influence of height begins at 16,500 feet, a height nearly coinciding with that of the highest pasture-grounds visited by shepherds."[1] Conway's party first became conscious of discomfort between 16,000 and 17,000 feet. Whymper's [2] expedition to the Great Andes of the Equator first felt real discomfort at 16,664 feet.

For healthy men in good training who take carefully chosen food we may therefore accept the Schlagintweits' limit as fairly accurate, while for people who are not in good condition, or who take food which they cannot digest, the limit may be very greatly lowered—a point which I will presently consider. This lower limit of distress in mountain climbing is therefore put wonderfully closely by the three sets of observers named. Whether it can be raised by prolonged residence at high levels is, I think, doubtful, and on this point it is not easy to obtain information of much value, seeing that in the absence of exact measurements observers may get so accustomed to what at first distressed them as to overlook it.

The symptoms of mountain sickness as described by a very large number of observers [3] may be stated as follows, keeping in mind that some only of them are noted by each observer :—

Those constantly met with are—great difficulty in getting enough air into the lungs, and a corresponding feeling of anxiety and distress, together with greatly increased dyspnœa and fatigue on exertion, with lassitude when at rest. The respirations are rapid, short, and gasping, and the ability for active exertion is much lessened, all these signs being met with in animals as well as in man. Common symptoms are palpitation of the heart, with a quickened pulse, severe headache, giddiness, singing in the ears, diminished appetite, nausea with or without vomiting, bleeding at the nose, and coldness of the extremities. Fairly common are indifference to danger, and loss of interest in things generally, often with a tendency to somnolence—although in some there is increased excitability—spitting of blood due to hæmorrhage from the lips, gums, air passages, or lungs. Bleeding from the conjunctivæ is sometimes observed, as also blurring of the sight, diarrhœa, and, in severe cases, muscular weakness so great that standing or sitting up is no longer possible; eventually the limbs become completely paralysed, then follows loss of consciousness, and perhaps death.

Curiously enough, lividity of the face, and especially of the lips, which must be familiar to every Alpine climber at great heights, is apparently overlooked by most writers or wrongly ascribed to cold.

The first question I have to consider is whether these symptoms are referable to one condition—viz., insufficient supply of oxygen, or whether this may be complicated by other conditions which require to be taken into account. If they be all due to dyspnœa or asphyxia alone they include phenomena which are not generally recognised by pathologists as possible results of imperfect supply of air, while if they be complicated with some other result of the rarefaction of the air, it is desirable that these possible complications should be clearly recognised.

How far do the known results of dyspnœa on the animal body correspond with the phenomena above referred to?

The gasping respiration we know well as the constant result of imperfect supply of air to the lungs when the air passages are unobstructed. We may equally safely put down the muscular weakness to imperfect supply of oxygen which we know is necessary for the contractions of the muscles.

The heart symptoms — viz., the palpitation and the acceleration of the rhythm—may safely also be ascribed to the dyspnœa. On arresting the respiration in the lower animals there is at first powerful vagus action, and the auricular beats soon become so weakened that the ventricles take on their own independent rhythm. It cannot in the meantime be proved that this causes the subjective feeling of palpitation of the heart, and it can only be said that the independent ventricular contractions show themselves under conditions similar to those which produce the feeling of palpitation of the heart, and that the latter is just the kind of feeling one would expect when the heart changes its mode of contraction in this particular way. In asphyxia as produced in animals there is a very great dilation of the ventricular walls, although the strain upon them (measured by the amount of blood pumped out *plus* the pressure in the aorta and pulmonary arteries) may not have been increased, and which is almost certainly due to the diminished amount of oxygen in the blood which circulates in the coronary arteries.[4]

This weakening of the heart brings the vagus mechanism into increased activity, the effect of this on the heart being to economise its action; and palpitation, if I am right about its nature, is under the circumstances an indication that the heart is distressed.

The cardiac dilation due to asphyxia is aided by the dilation which is caused by muscular exertion, and the two together will lead to heart-failure more readily than one of them singly; by heart-failure being understood the condition in which from extreme dilation the tricuspid valve can no longer close the tricuspid orifice.

There is no doubt that heart-failure is of not uncommon occurrence even in the Alps,[5] and that when it occurs the person suffering from it is practically incapacitated from further climbing, with intense dyspnœa, palpitation, and irregularity of the heart. Guides, who know the condition perfectly well in their own cases, or in that of their "Herren," have told me that when badly taken with it near the top of a mountain, the only way to get the person up the last 100 feet or so is to practically carry him up. The incapacity for further exertion is certainly very great, as I happen to know, but I should think that a quarter of an hour's rest would do just as well as carrying, seeing that recovery takes place in ten minutes or so, although at first sitting down gives no relief to the distress.

I now come to the other symptoms of mountain sickness, and have to consider how far they can be looked upon as due to asphyxia. The headache, with a sense of fulness, as if a tight band were drawn round the head, may be safely put down to cerebral congestion, and the hæmorrhages from the nose and conjunctiva agree with the known fact that the blood supply of the latter usually goes with that of the brain. Cerebral congestion is a constant result of asphyxia.[6] The giddiness, nausea, vomiting, blurring of the sight, and the indifference to danger, somnolence, and perhaps also the excitability, are all, I imagine, caused by the diminished supply of oxygen to the brain, which is perfectly compatible with congestion of that organ if the tension of the oxygen in the blood be reduced. The nausea and vomiting are of cerebral origin, for they do not cease with evacuation of the stomach, although they may follow the ingestion of food, and may become more marked as a result of indigestion. The lessened appetite and power of digestion are presumably due to the anæmia of the digestive tract, which is invariably produced by asphyxia, according to observations (by Roy and Cobbett), which are as yet unpublished. The singing in the ears may be due in part to difference in pressure of the air within and without the tympanic membrane, the eustachian tube not completely fulfilling its function in this respect.

The muscular weakness I have already referred to as due to the imperfect supply of oxygen to the muscles. The ready cooling of the extremities which prevented Conway's party from moving by moonlight at high altitudes I am inclined to put down to the diminished heat production, which results from the imperfect supply of oxygen to the muscles, which are the chief sources of heat in the body, and which may be aided by congestion of the skin increasing the amount of heat given off by it.

So far as the symptoms are concerned, we need therefore be in no difficulty regarding the nature of mountain sickness. It is asphyxia. The important feature in the asphyxia of mountain sickness is the reduction in the amount of oxygen supplied to the tissues, but the same effect is produced if, with a limited supply of oxygen to the system, there be from any cause an increased demand for it by the tissues. Muscular exertion is the most familiar example of this, and the greatly increased distress which results from attempts at active movement, is one of the features of mountain sickness. There is another cause of increased demand for oxygen by the tissues which is of importance in connection with mountain sickness, viz., fever. This is well illustrated by Whymper's experiences on Chimborazo (*loc. cit.*), where at a height of 16,664 feet he and two others of his party had an alarmingly acute attack of what they considered mountain sickness. This came on suddenly after a meal, one member of the party being, however, unaffected. Those affected felt feverish, with thirst, and had intense headache and extreme dyspnœa. These symptoms lessened a good deal next day, and two of the party were able to climb on the third day. No such intense distress was experienced by any of them on climbing more than 3,000 feet higher. Whymper recognises that this attack must have had a temporary cause, but he appears to have overlooked the fact that fever is not present in true mountain sickness, and that in all probability it was a case of poisoning with putrid food. Whymper mentions that some of his tinned meat had gone wrong, and it is curious that he should have overlooked the possible connection of this with the attack from which he and the Carrels suffered on Chimborazo. The serious symptoms of asphyxia are only what would naturally be expected to accompany any rise of temperature of the body at high altitudes.

Conway's observation that more distress was experienced in hollow places than when walking on an arête confirms what has been noted by others. This may be due to the fact that water takes up more oxygen than nitrogen from the air, so that when on a high peak the sun falls upon the snow, melting a certain part of it, the neighbouring air is robbed of some of its oxygen. The wind on a ridge need not have passed over fields of melting snow, and may therefore contain a larger percentage of oxygen. The difference in the amount of oxygen compared with nitrogen which water obtained from melting ice takes up is not very great, and the fact is probably not of much importance; but seeing that the two gases will not be dissolved in the proportions in which they exist in the atmosphere, but will each be dissolved as if it were the only gas present, we may have, even if the melting snow takes up equal volumes of oxygen and nitrogen, a very serious lowering of the percentage of oxygen in the air which rests or passes over the melting snow. This offers, to my mind, a very probable explanation of the increased distress noted by Conway in hollow places, especially when the sun was shining on them. Conway does not in his notes refer to variation in the degree of distress with the direction of the wind, but this is a subject which was much noticed by the Schlagintweits, and by numerous other observers, who found that they were most distressed when there was a wind from some particular direction. There is no reason for supposing that this was due to temporary variations in the barometric pressure, as such an obviously possible explanation could not have been very easily overlooked by the Schlagintweits. It is certain that air which has passed over a large area of snow melted by the sun will have suffered a diminution of its oxygen. If this idea be correct, such winds ought to be most distressing in the afternoon, when the quantity of water set free by the melting of the snow is greatest. On being frozen again at nightfall, the melted snow will give off relatively a large proportion of oxygen, which may explain why Conway and his party felt so much better at night.

It is possible that the increased distress felt by Conway and others in sunshine as compared with shade or cloudy weather was in part due to the increased demand for oxygen by the body when warmed by the sun's rays. Another point that strikes one in going over the literature of mountain sickness is that sometimes, especially in the Andes, dangerous symptoms show themselves at altitudes below 17,000 feet in persons riding on horse or mule-back, and where, therefore, there is no question of over-exertion. I have been at pains to follow out some of these cases, and find that previous attacks of malarial fever are recorded. The diminished amount of hæmoglobin in the blood which follows malaria will in these cases readily account for the asphyxia which shows itself, and may cause death in men and animals at heights below 17,000 feet.

I now come to the real gist of the matter, the one which Clifford Allbutt hoped would be decided by Conway's observations with the sphygmograph, namely, whether heart-failure is an essential element—indeed the essential element—in mountain sickness. Asphyxia, from whatever cause, can produce cardiac weakness and dilation, while, on the other hand, heart-failure, owing to the imperfect circulation, and therefore aeration of the blood, is a common and well-recognised cause of dyspnœa or asphyxia. If dyspnœa or asphyxia leads at altitudes of between 16,000 and 17,000 feet to heart-failure on moderate exertion, a vicious circle is produced, since the asphyxia tends to produce heart-failure, and *vice versâ.*

If this be the case, the limits of mountain climbing, as regards height which can be reached, become more restricted than would be the case if we had to deal with asphyxia alone.

To explain the point about heart-failure more clearly, I may state that the heart is a pump, which must pass on in healthy man or animals an amount of blood, which varies greatly at different times, in order to meet the requirements of the system as a whole. If the heart's work (expressed by the quantity of blood passed on, and the hydrostatic pressure against which this blood is expelled) be increased beyond a given limit, the heart as a pump becomes inefficient from dilation of the ventricles, so that the valves between them and the auricles can no longer close completely. This inefficiency of the cardiac pump can be produced in two chief ways. Firstly, by increasing the work thrown upon the heart; and, secondly, by diminution of its power. This latter can be produced by a great many causes, one of which is imperfect supply of oxygen to the organ. Others are, alcohol, tobacco, tea, disease of the heart, &c. Increase of work is produced by muscular exertion, fever, mental excitement, &c., &c. Any one of all the above causes is capable of itself of producing heart-failure. In most cases two or more of them are combined. For example, there can be little doubt, from the observations of Clifford Allbutt and others, that many of the cases of mountain sickness which occur at low altitudes, and which have so often been described in the Alps and elsewhere, are really cases of heart-failure from over-exertion and imperfect training, combined, perhaps, in some cases with errors in diet.

Indeed, heart-failure which cannot be distinguished from

true mountain sickness may occur at the sea-level. The point I have to consider, then, is how far Conway's observations and pulse-tracings indicate whether or not, while suffering from true mountain sickness, there was also heart-failure.

I give here reproductions of the pulse tracings of Conway and his party, taken at different altitudes, having chosen twenty-one of the total twenty-seven curves which have been submitted to me, those omitted being taken at lower levels than those shown, and being therefore of less interest in the present connection. The letters to the left of the figures show from whom each tracing was obtained, and the numbers give the pulse-beats per minute, which I have calculated from the rate of movement of the clockwork used to move the paper past the point of the recording lever. The descriptions to the right of the figures are Conway's notes. I will analyse the tracings briefly, without seeking to confine my remarks to the question as to whether they do or do not indicate that heart-failure is an essential element in mountain sickness, and I make allowance for the inaccuracy of the sphygmograph employed.

Pulse Tracings, all in Year 1892.

C. 84.
Mc. 78.
R. 112.
E. 96.

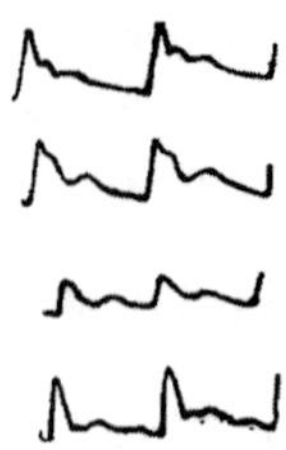

Fig. 1.

April 23, 2 p.m. Burzil Kote, about 12,000 ft. A day of rest in camp in miserable weather, snowing.

C. 144.
Mc. 126.
R. 120.
E. 126.

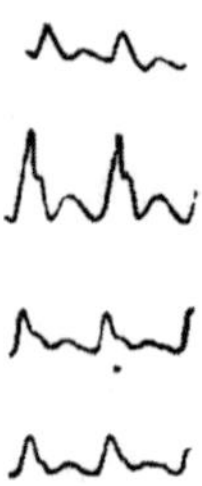

Fig. 2.

April 24, 2 p.m. Burzil (or Dorikun) Pass, about 14,000 ft. Tracing taken three-quarters of an hour after reaching col, after five hours of laborious ascent in deep snow. Several of the servants were badly affected to-day who gave no signs of suffering at much higher altitudes later on. All of us probably in poor condition.

C. 80.
Mc. 90.

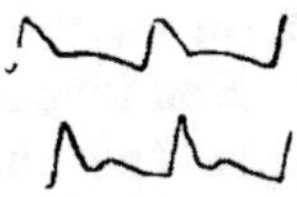

Fig. 3. Aug. 15, 10.30 a.m. In a snowstorm. We were resting in the tent all day at Junction (Throne glacier) Camp, about 16,000 ft.

C. 100.
Z. 90.
Mc. 78.

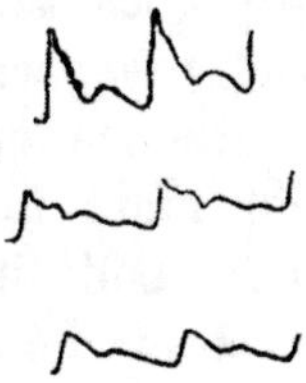

Fig. 4. Aug. 19, 7.30 p.m. After a day of rest at Footstool Camp, about 17,000 ft.

C. 90.

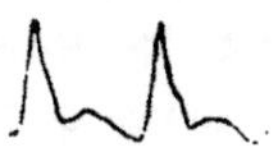

Fig. 5. Aug. 21, 11.30 a.m. Quarter of an hour above Serac Camp, about 18,000 ft. After a morning's severe climbing. Fine weather.

C. 99.

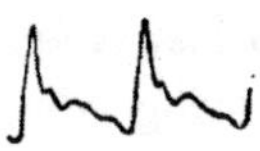

Fig. 6. Aug. 22, 6.40 a.m. Serac Camp (about 18,000 ft.). After a night's rest. Fine weather.

C. 102.

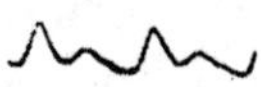

Fig. 7. Aug. 23, 2.15 p.m. Lower Plateau Camp (about 19,000 ft.). After a morning's climb, followed by several hours' rest. Fine weather.

C. 48.

Fig. 8. Aug. 24, 10.30 a.m. Upper Plateau Camp (about 20,000 ft.). After a morning's climb (when we were nearly frost-bitten) and two hours' rest.

C. 96.
Z. 100.

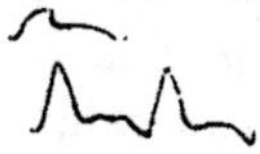

Fig. 9. Aug. 25, 3 p.m. Top of Pioneer Peak (about 23,000 ft. After eight hours of climbing with a few rests.

C. 96.

Fig. 10. Aug. 25, 4.30 p.m. Water Col close to second summit (about 22,000 ft.). After thirty-five minutes' descent from highest peak.

C. 72.

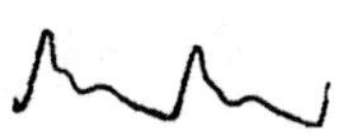

Fig. 11. Aug. 27, noon. At Footstool Camp (see Fig. 4). During a day of rest and bad weather.

C. 78.

Fig. 12. Sept. 1, 7.30 p.m. At Corner Camp (about 13,000 ft.). After a day's rest.

Of the curves in Fig. 1, Conway's and McCormick's are ordinary tracings of healthy men, such as one usually gets with a Dudgeon's sphygmograph, and the pulse-rate is within the usual limits of quiet life. Roudebush's and Eckenstein's show a more rapid beat, with the change in the form of the pulse-wave which usually goes with it.

Fig. 2 shows that the four members of the party were fatigued, the quick pulse-rate in the absence of fever indicating a demand by the tissues for more blood. I cannot go over the reasons which exist for believing that the "nervi accelerantes cordis" have for their function to increase the force and frequence of the heart in response to demands of the rest of the body for more nutriment,[7] and need only note that the form of the curves corresponds with the increased rate of heart-beat. It can be seen, however, that at the elevation of 14,000 feet the hearts of the four individuals concerned were beating very rapidly indeed—more than was the case with the same persons when they had climbed 8,000–9,000 feet higher. From this I conclude that fatigue or excitement (probably the former) rather than the rarefaction of the atmosphere is the cause of the quick pulse-rate which has been associated with mountain sickness.

Figs. 4–12 show that at heights of 17,000–23,000 feet the heart-beat need not be greatly quickened. Acceleration of the heart in mountain climbing is a measure of fatigue or nervous excitement, rather than of asphyxia from rarefaction of the air, which is a matter of considerable interest, since it indicates to us that when the "nervi accelerantes cordis" are called into play, it is not the want of oxygen but of something else that brings their reflex mechanism into activity.

Fig. 3, showing tracings taken at 16,000 feet, shows nothing abnormal in the form of the pulse curves. Fig. 4, at 17,000 feet, shows curves which one may get any day at sea-level.

Fig. 5, at 18,000 feet, cannot be called at all unusual. Fig. 6, at the same height, may be called a good healthy pulse. Fig. 7 is more dicrotic than is usual, but is not abnormal. Fig. 8, at 20,000 feet, with a fall to 48 heart-beats per minute, shows vagus action, the ventricles missing every alternate beat of the weakened auricular contractions. It is one form of the pulse of a distressed heart, and the form of the wave corresponds. Fig. 9, in Conway's case, looks like an anacrotic pulse-wave, which is generally associated with high arterial pressure—although by no means necessarily so; but in any case Zurbriggen's tracing at the same height is not one of high pressure. Figs. 11 and 12 are of not unusual form, and the rate of heart-beat is slowed down to about the normal in unfatigued individuals.

It may be said at once that these tracings do not enable us to decide the question as to whether heart-failure is or is not an essential element in mountain sickness. Two of them show unmistakably increased vagus action on the heart, but the others show rather evidence of fatigue than anything else. The vagus action is a sign of a distressed heart, and is usually if not always present in heart-failure, but it is often enough brought into play long before the heart has become overstrained. The palpitation of the heart which is so commonly noted in mountain sickness and exertions is, as we have pointed out, another sign of a distressed heart. It must be remembered that the tracings were taken during periods of rest, when the rarefaction of the air, and the consequent diminution of the oxygen in the blood, was the only influence tending to weaken the heart.

During such periods of rest the comparative regularity of the tracings is against the likelihood of failure of the heart at such times, and this is pretty well all one can say about them. They do not, and they cannot, enable us to decide definitely whether the heart is overstrained *during the exertion*, which is a necessary part of mountain climbing. I know of only one means by which this important question can be definitely decided, and that is by using a stethoscope, and learning whether or not a heart-murmur accompanies the first sound of the heart during exertion. If it does, we may diagnose functional incompetence of the mitral or tricuspid valve, or both, and therefore the failure of one or both ventricles; if the murmur be not present under these conditions we must in the meantime exclude heart-failure.

While thanking Conway most cordially for all he has done in the past in adding to our knowledge about mountain sickness, I would venture to ask him, when next he goes mountain climbing above 17,000 feet, to purchase before leaving England a binaural stethoscope, and get some medical friend to put him in the way of recognising a heart-murmur, and to use this stethoscope on himself and others of the party during or *immediately* after exertion.

There is only one other point and I have done, and that is the question how far, judging from the observations and tracings which are reproduced above, Conway had reached the highest climbable altitude. During rest at least, even at 23,000 feet, the curves indicate, on the whole, that muscular fatigue and distress of the heart were present rather than the nearly complete collapse of muscular power which accompanies well-marked heart-failure with the vagus slowing and irregularity. There is, therefore, no obvious reason why Conway and his party should not have gone higher, if they could do it quietly enough, and if they could choose their own times for going on and camping, &c., which of course is the real difficulty. The curves show that they were in a condition to go on, and they agree with Conway's own feeling that they had not come to the end of their tether.

CHARLES S. ROY.

CAMBRIDGE, *August* 25, 1894.

REFERENCES.

1. "India and High Asia," by H., A., and R. de Schlagintweit. Vol. ii. p. 484, London, 1862.
2. "Great Andes of the Equator," E. Whymper, London, 1892.

3. For literature up to 1877, *vide* "La Pression Barométrique." Paul Bert, Paris, 1877.
4. "Contributions to the Physiology and Pathology of the Mammalian Heart," Roy and Adami. Philosophical Transactions. Vol. clxxxiii. [1892] p. 284.
5. T. Clifford Allbutt, St. George's Hosp. Reports, 1879.
   "On Heart Overstrain," Roy and Adami.
6. *Loc. cit.* (4).
7. See Roy and Sherrington in the "Journal of Physiology." Vol. xi. p. 85.